"Like few pastors I've known, Doug has learned and grown from the toughest of life's lessons. He shares the experiences of loss and triumph in a writing style that is as approachable as he is. Doug has a theological understanding that probes deeper than many ministers' because he's been through the fire. I recommend you journey with Doug."

Philip Yancey, author

"As I read Doug Herman's book, I found myself desperately wanting to share it. He said what I have been wanting to say, trying to say, to two dear friends who have experienced two very different kinds of agonizing loss. This book is needed.

"This is not so much a story of one man's unspeakable loss as it is a journey experienced, not always in faith, but sometimes with a deep longing for faith. It is written with an honesty that will, at times, cause the reader to wince.

"Doug Herman's journey ends in forgiveness—of himself, of others, and in the ultimate miracle of our forgiveness by God, which allows us to get on with living in this world as children of God."

Tony Campolo, speaker and author

"As I finished the book, I felt hope. Tragedy is not the final word. The life of a believer does overcome—it's stronger than all the bad anger that tragedy provokes."

Dr. Larry Crabb, author

"When it comes to pain, grief, and its subsequent faith testing, those truly qualified to counsel are those who've endured tough trials themselves. Doug Herman's first-hand encounter with a seemingly silent God in the face of near insurmountable grief gives . . . honesty and insight like few others."

Steve Arterburn, author, director of New Life Clinics

"Doug identifies the struggle that I have had holding on to my faith in the face of painful experience. Most importantly Doug encourages me to trust God when I don't feel like it, when I can't find hope, and there are no explanations to relieve my pain."

Bryan Duncan, singer/songwriter

FAITHQUAKE

Rebuilding Your Faith after Tragedy Strikes

Doug Herman

Baker Books

A Division of Baker Book House Co
Grand Rapids, Michigan 49516

© 1997 by Doug Herman

Published in 2003 by Baker Books
a division of Baker Book House Company
P.O. Box 6287, Grand Rapids, MI 49516-6287
www.bakerbooks.com

Previously published by the author

Printed in the United States of America

Library of Congress Cataloging-in-Publication Data is on file at the Library of Congress, Washington, D.C.

ISBN 0-8010-6434-1

Scripture is taken from the HOLY BIBLE, NEW INTERNATIONAL VERSION®. NIV®. Copyright © 1973, 1978, 1984 by International Bible Society. Used by permission of Zondervan. All rights reserved.

The author is represented by Alive Communications, Inc., 7680 Goddard Street, Suite 200, Colorado Springs, Colorado 80920.

Contents

Preface

While *phenomenal* may be the word that best describes my life story, I have chosen not to write of the phenomena. Rather, I want to share with you some of the truths learned as my faith was forged on an anvil of seemingly unbearable events. Heart-gripping stories are abundant and, while stirring for a moment, of little eternal value. Truths are forever. They are absolute. They help us pound out convictions on which we can live our lives. This book reveals my years of hammering and the truths that survived.

Some time ago, I met a young television producer who described to me a concept for a program called *Day 41*. The title refers to the season of refreshing that follows a season of hardship as illustrated by biblical folks, some of whom were a lot like you and me. Noah endured forty days and nights in a turbulent storm. Moses spent forty years on the backside of a desert. Jesus spent forty days in temptation. For all of them, as for us, I've learned, when endurance has spent itself, fresh winds of change usher in day 41, a time of strengthening and encouragement.

In these pages I share the path that took me through—and beyond—some of life's darkest valleys. It's a well-blazed path, by no means unique to me. Footprints lay before us, left by one who experienced hurt beyond our comprehension. They lead to a place of healing and hope and show us the way to day 41.

The footprints in the valley of the shadow are those of Jesus Christ—and they're your size.

> To this you were called, because Christ suffered for you, leaving you an example, that you should follow in his steps.
>
> 1 Peter 2:21

Part 1

SURVIVAL
TECHNIQUES

"Our hearts will always smile through tears as we look back at the memories with Evon and little Ashli. Yet they leap in great joy as we realize that these two await our arrival in glory."

Doug and Josh Herman

1

My Own Faithquake

Your Father in heaven . . . causes his sun to rise on the
evil and the good, and sends rain on the righteous and
the unrighteous.

Matthew 5:45

We walked cautiously toward the hospital conference
room. I opened the door for my wife and one-year-old
son. Evon and I exchanged worried glances. Joshua,
with his hands in ours, seemed oblivious to any poten-
tial threat. But the call we had received had shaken our
nerves.

It had been a typically hot, humid summer day in Dal-
las when the phone rang. Evon shut off the vacuum
cleaner and answered in her usual upbeat voice. I
watched as her face quickly clouded. When she hung
up, she said our doctor wanted the three of us to come
in for a private consultation. Two weeks earlier, Evon
had been asked without explanation to come in for some

tests. Now the serious tone of our doctor's voice sur-
prised us. *Certainly this can't be life threatening,* we
thought. *We have given our lives to the ministry. God
wouldn't do that.* We were neither optimistic nor terri-
fied. Our faith in God's provision and protection was
solid. We were obedient, steadfast, somewhat numb . . .
but concerned.

Seated at the table were my wife's gynecologist and a
new doctor—an infectious disease specialist. After intro-
ductions the specialist began, "Mr. and Mrs. Herman,
in our testing of donated blood, we have discovered that
one of the two units of blood given Evon after your son's
delivery has tested positive for the HIV virus. This virus
will probably cause AIDS." After a seemingly eternal
pause, he added, "Evon has tested positive as well. I'm
afraid there is no cure."

We sat in stunned silence. The only words we could
manage were unspoken, expressed between our tightly
clasped hands. Both doctors told us about the lack of
information concerning this virus and its accompany-
ing disease. In July 1986 research on AIDS was in its
infancy. Medical professionals could do little to ease suffering or slow the progress of the disease. The doctors
recommended precautions to maintain a "safe distance"
between the members of our family and from our
friends. They cautioned against conceiving more children. They warned us to tell no one for fear we might
be ostracized.

Our secure little family seemed invaded, yet alone.
Evon and I still couldn't manage words.

I could only think, *You're talking to the Herman family here! Good people! We're from Hastings, "Hicksville,"
Nebraska. We can't have the AIDS virus. We've never used
drugs or been unfaithful. We don't deserve this!*

Fear crept in. *We've been married for only four years. Evon is going to die. And what about Josh and me—will we die too?*

Finally I thought of God: *I'm a minister! God doesn't call someone into the ministry just to wipe him and his family out, does he?*

This can't be happening!

Warning: Faithquake at Hand

Evon and I had moved to Waxahachie, Texas, in the spring of 1984. Children had been part of our dreams since our high school courtship and fall wedding in 1981. I was drawn by Evon's bubbly personality and the bright blue sparkle in her eyes and couldn't wait to see her Irish zeal passed on to our children—at least three or four of them. We had lived in Grand Island, Nebraska, for the first year of our marriage, then moved to Hastings where I worked for my father. After two years there, we felt the call of God to the wide open spaces of Waxahachie for Bible school so I could study to become a minister. Preparing for full-time ministry and eager to begin our family, we felt life was full of exciting changes.

Shortly after our move, we discovered Evon was pregnant. On February 19, 1985, I stood by her hospital bed (except for the two times I fainted) and watched as she delivered our first child. Exhilaration coursed through me. We had a son! After holding Joshua Ryan in the nursery, I returned to Evon's side. She was still bleeding from the delivery, but I assumed this was normal. We were both too ecstatic to question anything. The doctors gave Evon two units of blood and sent her to recovery. Two days later, I brought my wife and little boy home from the hospital.

Life was absolutely grand. The American dream? We were standing in its doorway!

As we settled into parenthood, classes at the Bible college kept me quite busy—but no busier than a growing, crawling, eating, messy little boy did. We loved our son and our new lives. We knew the future held phenomenal things for us.

Then came the call that seared our lives and happy visions. Evon's test results confirmed her HIV-positive status, and now they wanted to test me. It had been more than a year since Joshua's delivery—more than a year of unprotected intimacy. And since Joshua had been breast-fed, the doctors wanted to test him as well.

My first "faithquake" was fully in motion.

Riding the Richter Scale

Tests showed that Joshua and I were not infected. Though a huge relief, the news didn't erase the danger we still faced. Evon brought up issues of intimacy. "I don't want to orphan Josh, honey," she said. "If you and I both get the virus—if we both were to die—that wouldn't be fair to him. I want you to use precaution, and I want us to be careful—very careful."

I wrestled with these issues. I had begun to hope for Evon's healing. Was using condoms as protection showing a lack of faith in God's providence? Was it living in fear? *What good is faith that isn't acted upon?* I wondered. I thought of the last year and a half of unprotected intimacy—God had not allowed me to get infected. Was that not proof enough that God would keep me?

Over the next month, we grappled with these questions. We wanted more children, but the risk seemed too great. One night, however, I took action. During a night of passion, I removed the protection, unbeknownst to Evon. I thought, *How dare we allow HIV's invasion even here, in our most private moments?*

Through a combination of love, faith, and presumption, we found ourselves in another pregnancy. Evon was hurt that I put myself at risk, and she was also shaken by the pregnancy. But she understood my heart—to walk by faith. Together we struggled with the issue of God's intervention and together hoped everything would be all right.

Once Evon was pregnant, however, we discovered a new facet to our faithquake: Not only do friends and relatives fear and avoid people who are HIV-positive, so do doctors. Call after call, we were rejected. Many shuffled us to clinics. Two weeks of heartrending phone calls finally produced a quality obstetrician.

Our first meeting with him was straightforward. He advised us that in all likelihood, our unborn child would contract HIV. He suggested an abortion. We refused to consider it. "If God wants to terminate this pregnancy, then he can do it," I said proudly.

Ashli Nicole, with her mom's big blue eyes and a wave of black hair, entered our family on November 4, 1988. What a blessing she was. She began to crawl and coo like other babies, showing no sign of disease. We believed God had rewarded our "faith" and preserved her.

As months went by, though I remained HIV-free, we were forced to admit that all was not well with Ashli. By the time she reached nine months of age, neurological regression had set in. She could no longer sit or hold her head up. The month before she turned one, all she could do was wiggle her hands and feet, scream, and cry. Close to her birthday, we admitted her to Children's Hospital with a digestive infection. HIV had begun to rear its ugly head in her body.

When Ashli tested positive, the news winded my soul. *Where is God?* I wondered. *Where was he at Evon's transfusion? Does he truly exist?* A tide of questions swamped my mind and sucked breath from my lungs.

I freely challenged God. *How can you stand by and watch?* I asked him. *Why are you allowing an innocent baby to suffer pain and imminent death? What kind of God creates to destroy?*

We had no answers to these questions. As we began sharing our situation with others, we found our questions were also overpowering to our fellow believers. While well-meant, their clichés, verses, and quaint sayings did little to relieve the pressure of our hearts' pain.

During those same months, Evon battled a chronic cough and shingles on her back and neck. Periodic illness became a way of life. While her symptoms didn't classify yet as full-blown AIDS, they revealed the activity of AIDS-related complex, or ARC. *How ironic,* I thought bitterly. The word *ark* had always symbolized God's promises. We had put our lives into his sovereign hands, and he had let us down.

More infections ripped at Ashli's little frame, and she lived at the hospital for several months. We didn't have time to assess the status of our faith at this point; we were too busy attending to Ashli, shuttling Joshua between home and hospital visits, and coping with Evon's illness. Finally, several months later, after a prolonged battle with a "Christian" insurance company, we were able to bring her home. Nurses lived with us six to ten hours a day, but any inconvenience was worth having Ashli home again. I remodeled the basement to serve as her new hospital room. We cautiously began to hope again.

For what? For the complete, supernatural healing of Evon and Ashli. It was all we *could* hope for. All our haunting questions and fears could be mended by God

17

with this one decision on his part. *What a testimony this could bring to our world today!* we thought. In this whirlwind of pain, pleas for healing became our only prayers.

While a tough year, the months of 1990 filed past with relative ease. In November we celebrated Ashli's second birthday and set our eyes upon the holidays. We soon compiled Christmas wish lists; mine was rather short. What I wanted for Christmas that year was to sit around the tree with my wife, son, and daughter, and . . . that was it. Due to health crises, we had never had a family Christmas.

To make sure this would occur, we took Ashli to the hospital for a blood transfusion, where she received blood products that would build up her immune system and aid her health over the holidays. After two days of transfusions, she was ready to come home. It was Christmas Eve. I was thrilled! My dream was in sight.

After readying the van, I called to Evon, "It's time to go!" She didn't answer. I ran up to our bathroom to find Evon white and shaking. "I'm scared, honey," she gasped. "I think I need to go to the hospital."

She was right. Her doctor admitted her with a severe flu virus. She couldn't come home for Christmas. Because her mom was sick, Ashli couldn't come home either—doctors feared she would contract the virus from germs in our home. The next morning, Josh and I sadly opened half the presents. At first Josh would open a gift and cry out, "Thanks, Daddy! Thanks, Mom—" When he realized she wasn't there, he fell silent. It was a solemn celebration.

In my mind I pictured millions of Americans who were all opening their presents. Did they understand how fortunate they were? Did they realize how profound was the simple gift of having their families together? I suspected many focused instead on the paper and packages, taking for granted what Joshua and I so longed for: a mommy and a sister at Christmastime. The unfairness bruised my spirit.

The Ten-Count

Two days later, Evon did get to come home. She shouldn't have—she was still a little sick—but she was a lot Irish, with the temper to prove it. Having taken all she could, she threw her blanket against the wall and voiced her desire to go home.

Little Ashli wasn't so strong. She suddenly came down with PCP—Pneumocystis carinii pneumonia—which often kills people with AIDS. Ashli stayed in the hospital the following week.

We decided to spend December 31, 1990, praying in the new year with some dear friends. With all the faith we could muster, we asked for time, for healing . . . for hope. Evon prayed. I prayed—for a miracle. We went home after midnight, exhausted but trying to believe for good things. At 2 A.M., I received a page. Ashli was having breathing trouble. I hurried to the hospital to sign consent forms allowing the doctors to drain her lungs with a syringe.

I spent the next two days there. Ashli stabilized. On January 2, I drove home to get Evon and Joshua so they could visit. Evon was weary and ill herself, but she hadn't seen her baby in more than a week and longed to hold her. Evon's wish was dashed when Ashli had to be rushed into ICU in respiratory alert. Doctors gave her a shot to still her motor functions and inserted a breathing tube. A "J-tube" ran into her stomach for feeding, and a Broviac catheter ran into her heart for medication. More tubes ran into her wrists and ankles.

Ashli was only two years old. When I saw her naked, intubated body, my heart shattered.

After a long and pain-filled evening, we said good night to Ashli and went home. Two days later, the phone again rattled our world. "Doug, you knew there would come a time when we would need to have a serious talk. Can you meet with us this afternoon?"

The Beginning of the End

Evon and I knew what those words meant, and we discussed our options. She was too weak to accompany me to the hospital, so I went alone. There I found the family conference room filled with Ashli's doctors, nurses, specialists, and social workers. All the faces were extremely solemn.

"Doug, we are at a crossroads," began the infectious disease specialist. "Ashli's condition has greatly deteriorated. Her lungs are virtually filled with fluid. The machines are on 100 percent oxygen." He paused. "Doug, we can give her two days of life using aggressive medication. But that is all we can do. Your choice is this: You can shut off the machines today. She will probably die in a couple of hours. Or you can keep her medicated, and she will suffer and deteriorate for about two days and then die."

Then these compassionate doctors and nurses began to cry.

"Doug, we need to know what you want us to do. It is your choice."

My choice. I thought about that with deep resentment. None of this was ever *my* choice. I didn't choose for Evon to get the virus. I didn't choose for Ashli to contract this disease. But now—*now* it was my choice.

For several minutes, I choked on my grief. My mind raced to a childhood memory. I remember taking my first leap off the high-dive board at the swimming pool.

It was enormously high and frightening. Walking to the edge of the board, I felt that all creation paused in astonishment, waiting for this young lad to jump to his death. My toes dangled over the edge of the board. I looked down. A sudden rush of new fear paralyzed my arms and legs. "Hurry up!" my audience shouted. "Are you going to jump or not?" Finally, heart pounding, friends screaming, I edged to the end of the board and jumped.

I felt the same paralyzing rush of fear in that conference room. One answer dictated death; the other, suffering. My tears ran freely as I remembered what Evon and I had decided. I told them we did not want Ashli to hurt any longer. I told them to remove the machine.

I asked them to wait until friends and family had said their good-byes. The meeting disassembled, and I called Evon. We wept together, feeling the deep pain of loss, for ourselves and each other. Evon was too weak to come to the hospital, so I asked a friend to go stay with her while this was happening. I promised to call when Ashli was gone.

Hours passed, and friends and family filed into Ashli's room to hug, kiss, and pray for her. Finally, it was my turn. On my way to the room, I looked up. "You say you are the Prince of Peace?" I asked God. "Well, you had better show up. I can't do this alone."

Opening the door to Ashli's room, I walked over to her tiny form. Leaning down to give her a kiss, I broke. I wept uncontrollably. I experienced a vast inner longing . . . remorse . . . helplessness . . . pain. Deep pain.

Whether Ashli could hear me or not, I do not know. But I tried to explain what was about to happen. The doctor would give her a shot to stimulate her motor functions. The breathing machine would be stopped and the tube removed. She would have a chance to breathe on her own.

"And if you want to fight to live," I whispered, "I'll fight death and hell with you, baby. But if you want to go home, that's okay too. I love you, Ashli." I couldn't say the word *good-bye*.

Ashli used to love for me to sing to her, so I tried to do it one last time. Caressing her face, I sang, "Jesus loves me, this I know. For the Bible tells me so. Little ones to him—" I couldn't sing the next word. I wept. At that moment, God seemed to say, "She belongs to me, Doug." I felt so weak and defeated. I wanted Ashli to know how much I loved her. "Ashli, I'm sorry about the pain. I'm sorry about the hurt, the suffering, and your short life. But," I told her, "I am not sorry you are my little girl. I'm not sorry we had two years and two months together. I'm not sorry that I love you. And I'm not sorry that I get to see you again in heaven someday."

I finally found the strength to stop crying. I leaned over my little girl and kissed her forehead. "I love you, Ashli. Good-bye."

I called the nurse in, and she shut off the breathing machine. Ashli took two breaths and died.

The Middle . . . and the End

A twenty-seven-year-old mother had to bury her daughter and choose a headstone. As anguished as we were, my wife was never more beautiful than the day of Ashli's funeral. My wife was gorgeous to me—not just physically beautiful, although she was that. She was stunning inside, as a person. Her inner grace and unquenchable faith glowed that day.

Evon remained gorgeous to me during the following months as she went from 105 pounds to 80. She was gorgeous as she lost a lot of her hair due to chemotherapy, went on a breathing machine in August 1991, and fought her way off. She was gorgeous as the side effects of AIDS caused her to lose her eyesight. And she was gorgeous to me when she was hospitalized with severe breathing problems and we had to have our dreaded talk.

"Evon, the doctors said that if you go on the breathing machine again, you will probably not make it off. But if you don't, you're going to fight this thing until the end. Honey, we are still praying for a miracle. But if it doesn't come, sweetheart, tell me what you want me to do. I'll be faithful to carry it out. What do you want me to do?"

After a thoughtful pause, Evon whispered, "Put me on the machine one more time. Give me one more chance."

Later that afternoon, she experienced respiratory alert and was rushed to ICU to be put on the machine. I briefly stopped the nurse. I knew this might be my last chance to talk with Evon on earth. Holding her, I said, "I love you, Evon. Thank you for ten years of marriage. For Josh and Ashli. Thank you for being a wonderful wife. I love you."

I gave her a kiss. They gave her a shot.

A few days later, I was again summoned to the family conference room. Same situation. Same crisis. Different hospital, doctors, and patient.

"Doug, you knew this day would probably come," the doctor said gently. Again I faced the terrifying choice: two days of suffering, then death, or two hours of suffering, then death. As I sat before the doctors with tears streaming down my face, a voice flashed through my mind. "Evon has fought the good fight of faith," it seemed to say. "She has run her race in life. There is now laid up for her a crown of righteousness."

I turned to the doctor. "Let my wife go home. I don't want her to suffer any longer."

Friends and family flooded Evon's room to say good-bye. Then it was my turn. I couldn't talk or sing. I wept and wept, my head on Evon's chest. Could she hear me? I don't know. I think so. A tear trickled down her cheek.

I asked four dear friends to stay with me as the machine was turned off. We prayed. Every time Evon struggled to breathe, I writhed in pain. Forty-five minutes after the machine had been removed, three of my friends suddenly jumped to their feet and began praying aloud fervently. It was as if a spiritual presence had entered the room. We were on holy ground.

For seventy minutes, we sought a miracle. We watched Evon as her spirit began to unzip itself from her body. We saw her heart rate flutter from 78 beats per minute to 188, then to 0. I placed my dear bride in the arms of her ever loving groom, Jesus Christ.

Evon died on September 9, 1991.

Immediately after her death, my friend Randy went with me for a short walk. My heart felt ripped open. I felt I was hemorrhaging spiritually.

"Read to me, Randy," I said. "I just have a hunger for the Word of God. Would you read to me?"

As he read, it was as if cool water poured over my torn and feverish heart. I felt a fresh healing administered by the Prince of Peace himself. Randy read on and on from the Book of Isaiah. The Holy Spirit washed over and over me.

Slowly I felt God begin to heal and reshape my broken life. He has never stopped.

2

First Aid for Victims
of Faithquake

Life can be counted on to provide all the pain that any
of us might need.

Sheldon Kopp

Many people would say they are prepared for trials in
their lives. I would have said it before my faithquake hit.
Like other believers, I felt that since I knew the Bible
pretty well and had years of serving my Savior behind
me, I could probably handle anything that came my way.
How quickly my life revealed otherwise.

When Evon and I faced the earth-shattering news in
the hospital conference room, we were as shocked as
anyone else would have been. The doctors' message was
simple and horrible: "I'm sorry, but your wife will die.
You and your son are also in danger." As we drove home
after that proclamation, the thought of what the future
held tore through my mind. I began to hear a strange,

viral voice: "I'm going to kill you, Doug," it said. "I'm going to kill your wife, you, and even your little boy. Where is your God now? You were innocent, and now you will die."

I thoroughly knew tactics in spiritual warfare and implemented them, but the voice haunted me—with valid questions. Where *was* God? Where had he been during that blood transfusion that would eventually kill my wife?

Early on, this tragedy invaded my thoughts, my choice of vocation, and of course, my family life. As I pursued my ministerial credentials, I struggled with my doubts about God's presence in the midst of pain. At home Evon grieved over leaving her little boy. We wept over losing each other. Adding to the emotional burden were the strict precautions we had to take so I would not contract HIV.

All the while, our faith was torn between the God of love we had known all our lives and the God who now seemed so unconcerned. Instead of standing strong, our faith quaked.

Something We Share

Evon and I had been two innocent teenagers from the Midwest with our lives laid out before us; now we were adults battling for love, life, health, and faith. We felt we were fighting alone, that no one had ever battled tragedy in this way before. But that was not true; this war has raged on for centuries. Pain and adversity are no respecters of persons.

Who is exempt from adversity and tragedy? No one. I have ministered to thousands who have seen their lives explode in painful circumstances. I see their faces in libraries, churches, high schools, colleges, and shopping malls. I see the empty, hollow, distant look of those in need. Sometimes our eyes meet.

It happened recently on a plane to Chicago. A neatly dressed woman sitting across from me began a very innocent conversation. I really didn't want to talk. She obviously needed to.

"Are you from Denver?" she asked politely.

"Yes," I replied with a halfhearted smile.

"I was just visiting. I'm from Illinois."

"That's nice."

"I was visiting a good friend in Boulder. Poor thing. Her twenty-two-year-old son just passed away. It was all so amazing. He was playing basketball with some friends. Went up for a rebound and fell to the ground with a heart attack. He just died! He had never been sick. No history of medical problems. No aneurysms. Twenty-two years old!"

As the woman paused, her shaken and wounded heart began flowing into my life. She asked, "What do you say to someone like his mother? It seems so unfair." She began to weep.

What *Do* You Say in the Face of Tragedy?

My heart went out to this woman and to her friend. By the time I had this conversation, I had experienced death in my own family, and I knew how lost and stunned her friend felt. I bet the mother felt as I had— life looked wonderful, and she was as prepared as possible for whatever came. Instead, though, what came was both unexpected and faith-quaking.

The truth is, no matter how prepared you think you are, tragedy arrives with a force greatly underestimated. You can take precautions toward physical safety in the event of a fire or flood. You can study CPR to help in a medical crisis, read up on wise investment choices to avoid financial upset, and lock all your doors and windows to hinder burglars. But you can find no techniques to learn, books to read, or actions to implement that can truly shield you from the impact of adversity. There is no escape from major emotional or spiritual pain.

It's no wonder that we find ourselves, like Christ, in our own Garden of Gethsemane. The cup of adversity is pressed hard against our cold, pursed lips. We must drink. Yet somehow, like Christ, we must find the strength and courage to face this reality and not only survive its blast, but become stronger, more loving, and purer because of it. This is quite a task, one that many fail to accomplish. But tackling the task starts here.

> When tragedy arrives, face it in its entirety. Don't run. **First Aid Tool**

I shared this with the woman on the plane. She could best help her friend at that moment by bringing her to face the death. As a true friend, she could be available to the grieving mother to talk about it as often as needed. I challenged her to accept her friend's normal reactions of anger and frustration. "Sometimes we just need someone we can scream with," I told her. "No matter what she says, stay by her side and refuse the easy way out: to lapse into denial and quote meaningless clichés. Hold her close in support, let her feel what she feels, and help her face the reality head-on, rather than try to escape it."

The woman had also asked me why. *Why?* I hear that question often. It reminded me of a past encounter in western Colorado.

On this particular evening, I was guest speaker at a church. I had shared from the heart of God. I portrayed the truth of his love and compassion in the midst of tragedy. By this time I had lost Evon and Ashli, though that didn't make the message harder to preach. It's always hard to convince people of the kindness of God when they most notice his silence. Many people that night, though, had responded to the comfort of Christ. The local pastor then took the pulpit.

"We are going to praise God!" he declared.

"Amen!" chorused the crowd.

"When I am in victory, I'll praise him! When I'm in the battle, I'll praise him! In health or in sickness, I'll praise him! Even if my sickly parents die, I'll praise him! Nothing will keep me from praising my God!"

As the crowd reverberated their agreement, I saw a young woman, crying, flee the sanctuary. Shortly afterward, an usher came to me on the platform.

"Someone would like to speak with you," he said. "Do you have a moment?"

Assuring him that was why I was there, I followed him into an office. There sat the young woman and her mother.

"Can I help you in any way?" I asked.

"Mr. Herman, how can my pastor say those things? How can he say that he will praise God if his parents die? He hasn't had to go through that. How can he say that?"

She began to cry openly. Her mother encouraged her to tell me what had happened just two weeks prior.

"We were coming home from the mall," she said. "My husband was driving our van, and our two young daughters were in the seats behind us. As we turned off the highway, suddenly a cab came flying around some cars. It hit our van broadside."

The woman burst into tears and continued. "My ten-year-old was knocked through the side window of the van. After the van stopped moving, I ran to find my kids. The nine-year-old was okay, but not her sister. I found her on the highway bleeding badly. I held her in my arms and shouted for help. Looking into her eyes, her head in my lap, I waited for help. None came. None came! I watched my daughter die, Mr. Herman. Tell me, how can my pastor say those things about death and praising God? He doesn't *know* the pain.

"And tell me, Mr. Herman, why didn't God intervene? Why?"

No Harm in Asking

I couldn't speak for the woman's pastor except to say I'm sure he wasn't making light of the pain of bereavement. Really he was encouraging the congregation to a healthy yet difficult course of action: Praise (or trust) God in the midst of pain. As for asking why, we've all done so. Yet we often feel guilty about it. Can we challenge God this way?

We'll explore more about God's answers in a later chapter, but for now let's concentrate on the asking itself. It is not wrong to ask God why something has happened. God has shown us through many Scriptures that he longs to hear from and bear the burdens of his people:

> Trust in him at all times, O people;
> pour out your hearts to him,
> for God is our refuge.
>
> Psalm 62:8

"Call to me and I will answer you and tell you great and unsearchable things you do not know."

Jeremiah 33:3

Cast all your anxiety on him because he cares for you.

1 Peter 5:7

"Come to me, all you who are weary and burdened, and
I will give you rest."

Matthew 11:28

God not only invites our questions, he promises
answers—of a certain kind: "If any of you lacks wisdom,
he should ask God, who gives generously to all without
finding fault, and it will be given to him" (James 1:5).
He has made himself and his wisdom available. We have
only to ask.

Does James guarantee that the wisdom we receive will
succinctly explain away all the mysteries of life? No.
Instead, he makes clear
that God is accessible and
responsive. This wisdom
that God promises brings
an understanding of both
God's purpose for us and his love for us—these are always
entwined. As we grow in this wisdom, we realize that even
hardship is a place where his love can be expressed.

First Aid Tool

Feel free
to ask God why.

Asking is the expression of the intellect's insatiable
hunger—that inner desire to know, to understand. Adam
and Eve started the questioning. After receiving but one
command from their Creator, they began to question.
Would he, as the serpent suggested, withhold from them
a good thing? "The fruit looks good—why not?" The rest
is our sordid, hopeful history of struggle, sin, and
redemption. Asking why is completely natural, from our
earliest moments on earth to now. God is not offended
by our wonder.

Jeremiah was a man who dared to ask why. He is an
inspiration to me, not because he too experienced sorrow and overcame it, but because he faced God with his
questions.

Many are familiar with Jeremiah as a man of God
who received this wonderful pronouncement:

"Before I formed you in the womb I knew you,
    before you were born I set you apart;
    I appointed you as a prophet to the nations."

Jeremiah 1:5

But how many are familiar with the "weeping prophet"
who challenged God?

Probably many years span the time represented by
chapters 2 through 11 of Jeremiah's book. He had delivered a message of judgment and repentance to a hard-
hearted people. They responded unfavorably, to say the
least. In fact they arose against Jeremiah. By chapter
12, Jeremiah has had it.

You are always righteous, O LORD,
    when I bring a case before you.
Yet I would speak with you about your justice:
    Why does the way of the wicked prosper?
    Why do all the faithless live at ease?

verse 1

I must admit, reading that verse causes a grin to
spread across my face. Who of us hasn't felt as Jeremiah
did? I'm freed by the realization that this long-standing,
faithful prophet of God actually voiced his misgivings.
I know I can too. God is not shaken when I ask why.

And God's answer? Not particularly satisfying in
terms of explanation. He simply reiterates his plan for
Israel, promising punishment and then compassion. So
it is with us. The freedom to ask God why does not give
us license to receive a complete explanation. Sometimes
asking is all the satisfaction we'll get.

That may not seem comforting, but it should be. Let
me explain. When I was sixteen years old, my father and
I had an intense argument. As I remember it, I expressed

my anger—briefly. Then it was Dad's turn—and his turn never ended. Though I don't remember the gist of the argument, I know I felt that his punishment outweighed my crime, whatever it was. I asked why. He responded with a passionate narrative about the wages of sin. Undaunted, I continued to ask why. He gave me more nonanswers. "I know, but why?" Finally, my father turned to leave the room. He responded wearily yet firmly, "Because I'm your father—that's why."

That is the same answer God sometimes gives us when we ask why. He doesn't stop to give us details or gain our approval. He is God, after all, the greatest father of them all. If anyone should be able to "get away with" that response, it's him. Because it really is enough of an answer when it comes from him.

3

The Calling

The God of all grace, who called you to his eternal glory
in Christ, after you have suffered a little while, will himself restore you and make you strong, firm and steadfast.

1 Peter 5:10

"Suffering is not for Christians today!"

We've heard this doctrine propagated from pulpits
across North America. Evon and I confronted it when
well-meaning people made well-meaning yet illogical
and actually cruel suggestions.

One Thursday afternoon, I gathered with other youth
pastors for pizza and planning. Before prayer I shared
Ashli's latest battles while at Children's Hospital in Denver. Afterward we parted and I headed for my van. A certain pastor (I'll call him Sam) stopped me. "Doug," he
began, "I know God doesn't want your family to be sick.
You've got to have faith. If you just have enough faith,
Ashli and Evon will be healed." Our "discussion" ended
quickly.

As I drove home, I wept from the sting of his words. *Do you think I want to see them die?* I asked silently. *I've done everything possible in faith to see healing. I know!* I thought. *Let's have you go through a catastrophe and see if you have enough faith to counteract it.*

Did Sam realize what he was suggesting? Probably not. He couldn't imagine serving a God who allows suffering, but God does. Another colleague and a close friend expressed a similar lack of logic. "It is not in the plan of God for man to die until he is seventy or eighty years of age," he said. "Hallelujah!"

Oops! I thought. *He had better go tell ten of the disciples and Jesus!*

Evon and I were inundated with books and tapes by evangelists and ministers who believed God never allowed suffering in his family. "Every good and perfect gift comes from God!" they preached. "Sickness and suffering are not good and perfect gifts. They are not from God. And if God didn't give them to you, you don't have to keep them." At the time that sounded logical to us. We read the books, listened to the tapes, and took Evon to national crusades for prayer—all to no avail. *If God doesn't want us to suffer,* I wondered, *why are we suffering? What are we doing wrong?*

After all we went through, I have to challenge such a doctrine. Life itself challenges it. If most (probably all) Christians suffer in some way, do we then conclude that none of them has enough faith to ward off his or her tragedy? Common sense, among other things, confirms that life is hard. Even Scripture guarantees tough times. Jesus himself said, "In this world you will have trouble" (John 16:33). The prophet Isaiah wrote of this when he warned, "When you pass through the waters . . . when you pass through the rivers. . . . When you walk through the fire . . . " (Isa. 43:2). Most specifically, Paul informed us that "the sufferings of Christ flow over into our lives" (2 Cor. 1:5).

Paul was right. What you and I have experienced is part of those sufferings. Some experience the rejection Jesus experienced. Some face the insults and hatred Jesus endured. And others of us undergo the emotional and physical pain he felt on the cross along our trek toward our eternal home.

You see, friend, we are *called* to suffering because our Lord endured it, and so shall we. It is part of our journey as disciples. The idea that we're called to experience pain is small if any comfort to those struggling through the aftershocks of a faithquake. But before you get too discouraged, wait—our calling is two-pronged. Pain isn't the end of the story for us any more than it was for Christ. Like him, we are called to pain, but then to comfort. Glory. Resurrection life. Scripture predicts suffering and promises comfort.

Read the rest of the verses listed earlier:

"In this world you will have trouble. But take heart! I have overcome the world."

John 16:33

"Fear not, for I have redeemed you;
    I have summoned you by name; you are mine.
When you pass through the waters,
    I will be with you;
and when you pass through the rivers,
    they will not sweep over you.
When you walk through the fire,
    you will not be burned;
the flames will not set you ablaze."

Isaiah 43:1–2

> For just as the sufferings of Christ flow over into our
> lives, so also through Christ our comfort overflows.
>
> 2 Corinthians 1:5

Peter says it most clearly in his first epistle. First Peter 2:13–20 spells out specific conduct appropriate to followers of Christ. Then Peter writes, "To this [behavior] you were called, because Christ suffered for you, leaving you an example, that you should follow in his steps" (v. 21). Look at that verse. Meditate on it. It says that Christ suffered for us. Was it so that we would never suffer? No! It was to leave us an example so we would know how to handle suffering when it came. Christ did not remove suffering. He provided a personalized path in it to glory.

How *do* we handle the pain of faithquakes? The way Jesus did. We are to follow in his steps. Jesus met adversity with sinlessness and trust in God (1 Peter 2:22–23); the humility of a servant (Phil. 2:5–8); submission to God's will and prayer (Luke 22:41–44); and determination to obey his Father (John 18:11). Suffering, then, is not all we can look forward to experiencing. "Through Christ our comfort *overflows*," Paul says in 2 Corinthians 1:5. Perhaps the most comforting thought we can have is that we are not alone. The path through confusion and pain has been trod before us, and we won't travel it alone.

Jesus' Pain

Even in the darkest of times, we are not alone. God will never leave us or forsake us (Deut. 31:6). Even though we may question his presence at times, he is faithful and true. Jesus knows faithquakes. He has experienced more shattering pain than we can even imagine. For only he has been truly alone.

"At the sixth hour darkness came over the whole land until the ninth hour. And at the ninth hour Jesus cried out in a loud voice, 'Eloi, Eloi, lama sabachthani?' [My God, my God, why have you forsaken me?]" (Mark 15:33–34). Do you hear the pain and loneliness in that cry? When Christ bore all of our sins on Calvary, a wall of sin shot up between Jesus and his Father. Jesus, who became sin for us (2 Cor. 5:21), was temporarily forsaken by a holy Father who could not abide with sin. It was the first time in all eternity that Jesus felt forsaken and alone. The depth of this pain is beyond human comprehension.

Friend, God will not leave you, because the only wall that could accomplish that, sin, has been taken away forever. He is close by in the midst of your pain and mine.

You may be thinking, *But, Doug, didn't you ever feel alone when your family was sick?* Sure I did, many times. How can I describe the isolation I felt as I drove away from Lutheran Hospital on so many nights, leaving my wife alone in her room? Navigating the chaotic boulevard, I seemed to move in slow motion. It was as if the pain of loneliness sent me into shock, leaving me numb.

I remember walking through a mall with Josh during one of those times. We walked and window-shopped. The liveliness of the mall was attractive and engaging. But the depth of my aloneness was amplified as I saw couple after couple walking in step, their arms entwined. How I hungered for Evon to walk that way with me as we had hundreds of times before.

Later, after Evon had been released from the hospital, she and I sat in a pancake house, one of our favorite places. We watched the other customers while we waited for our meals. They laughed, talked, joked. We felt out of place. In the midst of that jovial crowd, happiness seemed remote and something we once took for granted.

Yes, friend, I've felt alone. But the fact is, regardless of my feelings, I have never been actually alone. God doesn't forsake us.

The Spiritual American Dream

Despite the well-meaning messages we've heard for years, we know that Christians do indeed suffer and feel pain deeply. Christians also find the comfort of God in the midst of their tragedies.

The first half of this is not a popular truth. What we really want to hear is how God wants us to be rich, healthy, and happy. We want to hear how God always heals, always fulfills, and always prospers. In short, we want eternal life—on earth.

First Aid Tool

Trust in the fact of God's presence even while you're missing the feeling of it.

People often ask me about this. After speaking on this topic, I've been told, "I did not want to hear what you had to say because I didn't want to believe it to be true." "I can understand the part about our calling and suffering as Jesus did. But it doesn't seem fair that pain finds so many innocent victims." "What did your family do to deserve AIDS?" "Why does my son have leukemia [or cancer or . . .]?"

Time after time as my family and I battled crises in our lives, we found ourselves questioning the fairness of God. While we knew the passages in Scripture like those listed earlier, we felt as Job: We don't deserve this! This isn't fair. Bad things should not happen to good people.

My friend, it is painfully simple. Life is not fair. It never has been. Not since the Garden of Eden and the fall of man.

Philip Yancey writes about this in his book *Disappointment with God:*

> The primal desire for fairness dies hard, and it should. Who among us does not sometimes yearn for more justice in the world here and now? Secretly, I admit, I yearn for a world "fault proof" against disappointment. . . . But if I stake my faith on such a fault-proof earth, my faith will let me down. Even the greatest of miracles do not resolve the problems of this earth: all people who find physical healing eventually die. We need more than a miracle. We need a new heaven and a new earth, and until we have those, unfairness will not disappear.[1]

We cannot "pray suffering away." We cannot "build up enough faith" to alleviate adversity. Suffering is just as real as life itself, and it has been around since the fall of man. It was around Paul the apostle as well.

Paul's Pain

If anyone ever had reason to be bitter at God, it would have been the apostle Paul. This wonderful man of God was a magnet for pain and adversity. In his own words, he describes his life:

> I have worked much harder, been in prison more frequently, been flogged more severely, and been exposed to death again and again. Five times I received from the Jews the forty lashes minus one. Three times I was beaten with rods, once I was stoned, three times I was

shipwrecked, I spent a night and a day in the open sea,
I have been constantly on the move.

2 Corinthians 11:23–26

Paul may have had the same feelings you and I have—
"This isn't fair!"—and even more often. But this mature
man of God found that the hardships he experienced
qualified him for a completely different purpose in life.
Pain does not give license for criticism and judgment of
God. Rather, it provides an opportunity for the healing
comfort of the Holy Spirit to work in our lives. It's a per-
fecting work that qualifies us to minister to others.

Paul wrote the Corinthians a letter that explained this
principle. Notice the ministry and qualification for ministry he described in this powerful letter:

> Praise be to the God and Father of our Lord Jesus
> Christ, the Father of compassion and the God of all
> comfort, who comforts us in all our troubles, so that
> we can comfort those in any trouble with the comfort
> we ourselves have received from God. For just as the
> sufferings of Christ flow over into our lives, so also
> through Christ our comfort overflows. If we are dis-
> tressed, it is for your comfort and salvation; if we are
> comforted, it is for your comfort, which produces in
> you patient endurance of the same sufferings we suf-
> fer. And our hope for you is firm, because we know that
> just as you share in our sufferings, so also you share
> in our comfort.
>
> 2 Corinthians 1:3–7

In the midst of your pain, have you experienced the
comfort of the Holy Spirit? If so, you have been ordained
by Almighty God to bring comfort and salvation to those
enduring hardships themselves. You do not need to have
battled AIDS to minister to someone with AIDS. You

need only to have hurt and found the embrace of powerful and divine arms of comfort.

Let go of the struggle with unfairness so you can use
your energy in other ways. Know that your suffering is
not in vain. Use it to comfort someone else with the comfort you have received. It
will be healing for you
and the person in need.

Suffering is reality for
Christians today just as
it was for Christ himself.
Life was not fair to the
Son of God. Neither will it be fair to you or me. Yet, having endured all of life's pain and unfairness, God in the
flesh provided comfort in the presence of imminent suffering. Our Lord has upon his body the scarred evidence
of one who can endure.

Take courage! The light at the end of the tunnel is not
a train. If you find yourself in the valley of shadows, you
will find that you are following a set of footprints, and
you can count on his steady presence. Dear friend, follow in Christ's steps.

> **First Aid Tool**
>
> Share any comfort you've received. It's wonderfully contagious.

4

When "Why?" Becomes the Cry of Your Heart

If I have sinned, what have I done to you,
    O watcher of men?
Why have you made me your target?
    Have I become a burden to you?

Job 7:20

Why? Thousands of pounds of ink and paper have been used to try to answer that question. Yet it still burns hot in those facing loss. The scars this question seared into my soul are constant reminders.

In a two-month period, my entire life and faith came to a crashing climax. I had taken my infant daughter to the hospital for tests to determine whether or not she actually had the HIV virus that causes AIDS. Test after heartrending test, I came to the realization that she did. The news of her condition began a landslide of events that swept strength from my soul.

First, Ashli was an AIDS baby at just six months of age. During this same period, my grandfather—a wonderful Christian man—died of liver cancer. Then we found out that my youngest brother, Dan, had AML (acute myeloblastic leukemia).

My life and faith were assaulted.

I had had enough. God was supposed to be my refuge and hiding place! I was a minister! I had given him my life. It was time for God and me to have a face-to-face talk. Either God was big enough to deal with all my pain or he just wasn't big enough.

At two o'clock in the morning, I entered the church building where I was on staff. Numbly walking onto the platform, I wondered how I was going to address this silent God. Sitting at the piano, I tried to worship, but walls of pain loomed before me. Song after song, I tried to press toward the heart of God, but the picture of my family that I had brought with me seemed to shout a response: "He's not answering!" Somewhat defeated, I went to the podium. I leaned on the pulpit, holding my little black Bible. My body began to shake. I trembled inwardly as I quietly began to pray.

My heart ached with the burdens of our trials. Breathing itself had become a great effort. And, oddly enough, all the biblical studies, insightful lectures, and excellent training I'd received to earn my ministerial credentials proved little help now. I had to hear something personal from the God I faithfully served.

"Why? Why? *Why!*" I began to cry. Soon my cries turned to screaming. Hurt and anger rolled from my heart and mouth like a thick fog at the coast. In my desperation, I unloaded my heart. I yelled my pain and frustrations to the heavens. I groaned audibly to any ear of compassion that would hear. Throwing my Bible against the wall and myself onto the ground, I screamed all my hurt, all my anger, all my confusion, and all my heated pain to God.

"Why my grandfather?" I pleaded. "Why my brother Dan? I thought you called him into the ministry! He is only a junior in high school! It's not fair. Why my wife, Evon? I was the rebellious child; she wasn't. She's never done anything to hurt you. Are you taking my punishment out on her? I thought you were just!

"And why Ashli? She's only six months old! Can't you feel the pain? Can't you see her lying there? Are you God or aren't you? I thought you were my heavenly Father. I thought you cared about me. I thought you loved me! Why the pain? Why the death? Why don't you speak to me? *Why?*"

Weeping. Shouting. Questioning. Unloading my pain. For hours.

There was no response. No voice, either audible or still and small. No sound except the reverberation of my anguish off the pristine walls. Nothing but silence.

Fear of the Question

My experience raises two questions: (1) What good does it do to ask why? (2) What if God meets your question with silence?

Since these are weighty issues, we'll deal with the first query here and the second in the next chapter. We've discussed the fact that many of us have been brought up to believe that it is wrong to question God—that to ask why is an act of disobedience or irreverence. But most of us who have experienced a faithquake know what it's like to hurt so badly that we have to speak out our pain to God. As I mentioned in chapter 2, I've come to believe that God is not offended by our questions. He is indeed big enough to handle our pain.

Sometimes we in the ministry know too well what Scripture says about life and death. Sometimes we know all about sufferings and trials, tragedy and victories. We have all the answers neatly packed away in our custom-made theological "black bags." Like some type of spiritual pharmacists, we prescribe plenty of verses for the injured: "Read two of these and call me next Sunday."

As a minister, I had all the comforts of doctrine and tradition stripped from me. My faithquake peeled away the cozy cocoon of rituals that I never questioned. I was left with nothing but the skeleton of my faith—just enough to believe there was a God who would hear and answer my question.

My need to ask overcame my fear of what answer I might receive. I knew I could hear a harsh reproof as Job did. Even more frightening at that moment was the possibility I would hear nothing. Those of us who have spent years in theological study have at least a basic concept of who God is, what his character consists of, and how he responds to us. But what would happen to this theological foundation if I received a response contrary to my understanding of God? A response of silence—which is itself challenging to comprehend since we know that God hears every prayer—is the hardest to take.

By all means, ask. But ask right.   **First Aid Tool**

So is it any wonder that many of us do not want to ask God why? The response we demand may be one that causes even greater pain and uncertainty. How much easier it is to brush aside these questions and stick with the answers found in Theology 101.

Considering the "answer" I received, it's fair to ask: Is it worth asking why? Without hesitation, I would say yes. Asking why is important for many reasons. It keeps our communication lines with God open and functional.

It is honest, a quality God heartily endorses. It brings us to the core of a problem, clearing away the insignificant issues. In a faithquake, our tumultuous emotions have to go somewhere. Why not take them to the one who totally understands them? Asking why lays bare our faith and invites God's intervention.

In short, it does much good to ask God why, but we can do so in good ways or bad.

How to Ask

We can see from Job's account that "why" must be asked inquisitively, not accusingly. It must always be for the purpose of understanding rather than judgment. God is, after all, God. He doesn't owe us anything. He's given us more than we can repay or even fully appreciate. He deserves, at the very least, our respectful approach.

My son exemplified this approach one evening following a church service. Joshua was four years old at the time and full of questions. We were alone in the car when our conversation began.

"Daddy?" Josh asked, staring at the aspen trees as they raced by.

"Yes, Josh."

"Do trees go to sleep at night?"

"Sure they do." I could feel the next question. "And they don't even need pillows."

"Oh." He paused for a moment. "Daddy?"

"Yes, Josh."

"Why do we go on green and stop on red?"

He stumped me! *Think quick. Be creative.* "Because green is the color that stands for growth and going forward." Ha! Superdad strikes again.

"Oh. Daddy?" Tenacious for a four-year-old.

"Yes, Josh."

There was a thoughtful pause.

"Daddy, why are there gates in heaven?"

Whack! Right into my theology! Why *are* there gates in heaven? "Uh, because God made it that way, of course," I stalled.

"But why? To keep people out? Or to keep people in? Why are there gates in heaven?"

Though I didn't have ready answers for every question, this humorous interaction between an overstuffed theological intellect and an innocent young boy illustrates the way a child should ask why. My son didn't try to challenge my position as his father. Neither was he rebellious in his questions. His questions didn't offend me—actually they honored me. They showed his trust in me. They proved he knew where to take his curiosity when it stumbled him.

We should pose our questions to our Father God from this position of inquisition, not accusation. Questioning simple actions in life is not wrong. Neither is questioning God. After all, his Son did.

When Jesus Asked Why

Let's look at Jesus on the cross. In Mark 15:34 we find our beaten and bleeding King suspended in air by three nails. In extreme pain, he is surrounded by a crowd of people while drowning in a sea of loneliness. Once again he speaks, quoting Psalm 22. He is speaking from his heart. "My God, my God, *why* have you forsaken me?"

On the cross, did Jesus find stern rebuke from the heavenly Father because he asked this question? Of course not. Like us, he had to speak of his anguish to his Father. For the first time in all eternity, Jesus was experiencing the agony of separation from constant communion with the Father and the Holy Spirit. True aloneness and isolation engulfed him. He asked why from the position of pain—a position you and I, in differing degrees, know as well.

Did he receive an answer? Maybe, but Scripture doesn't record one. One thing, however, is certain. Jesus was soon to receive love, adoration, and acceptance— not chastisement—from the heavenly Father. We find no evidence that God disapproved of the question. Rather, I believe he understood and left Jesus' example as an encouragement to us.

Don't be afraid to ask why. God is not afraid of our questions, and as we shall see in the next chapters, he does answer.

5

Deafening Silence

He [Herod] plied him with many questions, but Jesus gave him no answer.

Luke 23:9

Let's return to the dark church where I barraged God with my questions. My faithquake had made my once-bright spiritual life as murky as the empty building I was in now. Maybe that is what your heart is like. At one time you experienced the fullness and exciting love and life of a happy, easy relationship with God. Now your heart feels dry. Like a dark church. Lifeless. Still.

I wept and screamed my questions at God for hours. Finally, I was still. I waited for an answer. Any response at all. I pleaded for a sign—anything. A popping noise. A shuffling. Even an angel. But there was nothing. Absolute, deafening silence.

Picking up my crumpled little Bible, I went home deeply disturbed. I questioned the love of God. How could he care and yet remain silent? Was he just sitting on his hands, observing our pain from a distance? I couldn't understand his lack of response. I wondered if he was even real.

If you're in a faithquake, you know what I mean. Silence hurts. It is part of our inner design to communicate with one another. We were created to communicate with our Creator. When we experience this drought of interaction, our inner being writhes in anguish and loneliness. When the silence comes from someone we love, confusion and frustration amplify the pain. I knew I hadn't lost God—that he would never leave me. But I missed his voice. All I wanted was to talk to him. And I wanted his response. To have him simply clear his throat would have been a welcome surprise.

That began three months of silence from God. When I prayed to him, I heard nothing. I sensed nothing in the form of the Holy Spirit speaking to me in that still small voice. Scripture seemed like rhetoric. For those months, I struggled to minister to others while experiencing excruciating spiritual pain. I was not "faking" the ministry; I was trying to survive. I *wanted* to believe. At times I wanted to quit because at these times I didn't believe. I didn't want to preach something I couldn't stand behind, but quitting wasn't an option. You see, my insurance was tied to my ministerial credentials. If I quit the ministry, I lost my insurance.

I remember going to the pulpit the Sunday morning after confronting God. Standing there in my crisp suit, I brightly announced to the congregation, "Welcome to the house of the Lord this morning! Would you stand with us as we sing. . . ." And I went through the motions. For three months, I went through the motions. As a minister. I'm not happy about it now, but at the time it seemed the only course of action.

We prayed for the sick. Songs of grace and divine love echoed in our auditorium as I led the congregation. We smiled and laughed and hugged each other. Yet no one knew my despair.

The Truth about Roots

The months I longed for God's voice taught me something that's best illustrated by a story. The story begins in one of my favorite places—my yard. I love the smell of fresh-cut grass and tilled soil. Looking over the colorful array of flowers, grasses, and rocks gives me happiness. I love the growth and even love the work it takes to make a beautiful yard. (Some of you are reaching for your phones right now to offer your yard work to me. Thanks, but my fetish is for my yard alone.)

Yard work is a type of therapy for me. I am that man on the block who manicures his lawn rather than cutting it. Yes, the lines have to look exactly right when I finish to give it that professional touch.

One summer I installed a sprinkler system. Two weeks after the installation, I found my perfectly trimmed lawn covered with mushrooms! While great for practicing my golf swing, it was not what I wanted. So I asked professional lawn companies for advice. "Don't water so much," they said simply, explaining that when you do so, not only does the lawn develop fungi like mushrooms, but it becomes damaged. It seems that grass, like most other plants, requires a season of drought. These dry spells cause the grass to drive the roots deeper into the soil in search of water. With deeper root systems, the grass becomes healthier and able to withstand more adversity.

So it is, I learned, with our spiritual lives. When I sought God with my whole heart and longed for him to speak to me, I experienced a "drought" of sorts. I know he wasn't mad. But this silent period of three months caused me to drive my spiritual roots deep into the soil of my beliefs. I began to examine everything I did and said as a Christian. I began to ask why I believe what I do. In my hungry search for God's existence, I examined all my long-held, innermost beliefs for reality and truth. I swam in Scripture and sought God in prayer—relentlessly.

The result was that my faith grew stronger than ever before. From this point on, I knew that what I believed was based on Scripture. My security grew from a relationship with God derived from conviction instead of emotion. When challenged with opposing doctrines, I was unshaken. Trials and temptations had impact, but due to the stronger roots of my faith, I was not moved. (More on the details of this search in chapter 9.)

First Aid Tool

Study to know what you believe and why. Let your roots grow deep in your search for God's truth.

Yes, this took time. Yet through all of my searching, I kept finding assurance. My "study in silence" confirmed to me that God's presence was as real as ever. I discovered through Scripture that many saints felt what I was feeling—yet God never let them down, and no matter how distant he seemed, he was never ignoring them. Think of Abraham, leaving his familiar surroundings for an undisclosed destination, then believing that God would bless him and his elderly wife, Sarah, with a son (Gen. 12:1–8; 18:1–15; 21:1–7). Abraham experienced the fulfillment of God's deliverance—as promised.

Hebrews 11 touches briefly on many lives of faith-filled saints. We love to read the exploits of Abraham, Enoch, Noah, and the others. But how often do we meditate on those listed in verses 35–38? These saints were tortured, stoned, sawed in two, destitute, persecuted, killed. Do you think they ever wondered when Christ would answer their prayers?

The Bible doesn't say it directly, but I think they often stood for their faith in the face of heaven's silence. Why? Because they died for their *belief*. This was intangible, not something immediate, touchable, and comforting. While I'm sure these martyrs experienced the presence of God, I'm sure they faced dark doubt as well. But their faith was real enough to them to die for.

Remember, too, how Jesus experienced God's seeming silence while on the cross. When Jesus cried, "Why have you forsaken me?" we don't know if God replied or not since no reply is recorded. In a sense, though, he did reply to Jesus, the same way he replies to you and me even when he seems silent. He spoke through his *actions*. He touched a dead body and made it supernaturally incorruptible. He empowered Christ to take the keys of death and Hades. He gave Christ a resurrected body, which proved to be a great comfort to the disciples.

God's answer—or lack of one—may not have seemed logical or sufficient at that point in time, but it makes perfect sense today. Jesus asked why. And as the clouds of pain and disappointment faded, the answer became bright and clear. Redemption for humankind was the reward. Again this wonderful, triune God excelled through tragedy to triumph. That is his specialty!

The same can be said for us.

Listen Closely—That's God Speaking!

Later I realized something about God's silence. It was only in retrospect that I could see he had never been silent at all. During those lonely months, people in our church expressed their love to me. They had said, "Are you okay, Pastor Doug? You've been on our hearts lately. We've been praying for you. Is everything all right? We love you, Pastor Doug. Is there anything we can do?" For three months, they reached out, and for three months, I slapped away their hands. I didn't trust them.

This only added to the emotional isolation I felt from God. No matter how dark things got, Evon and I kept our situation secret. We wanted to tell the congregation, and we needed their prayers, but we feared their reaction. How would they deal with the painful context of our lives shattering their stained-glass service? What would they think or do? We did not want to be rejected. Even more important to me was protecting my four-year-old son. I did not want Joshua to be ostracized for something he had no fault in. So we remained silent in our pain.

I realize now that in refusing their outstretched arms, I refused the body of Christ—the outstretched arms of Jesus himself. How I wish I had allowed those people to love me as the Spirit of God was prompting them. The fear of rejection paralyzed me into deafness. And I remained alone in my pain.

When I speak in churches, I find a common condition regardless of doctrine, size, or community status. A great lack of trust exists among Christians. Oh, I know we say we trust one another, to a certain point. But to entrust the fullness of who you are on the inside to another and allow yourself to be that vulnerable is tough. I understand. I didn't trust a soul.

First Aid Tool

No matter the circumstance, try to talk it out. Isolation wounds. Discussion often heals.

Jesus may be trying to speak to you and comfort you as well. He wants to love you through the outstretched hands of his body. But you will not be able to receive that love from Jesus or hear his voice unless you are also willing to accept it through the voices and love of the people around you. This is risky. We all have to choose our confidants carefully. But this is another way he desires to speak with us.

That said, I know some of you will respond, "Your experience was good, Doug. But I'm really alone. No one has reached out to me—God or man." I acknowledge that along some of the journey you may feel completely unnoticed and uncared for. Don't assume, as I did, that God withheld his presence. After all, he speaks in many ways.

You may also be experiencing spiritual drought right now. If you feel your prayers are bouncing off the walls—that God is there but waiting to act—take heart! Allow the roots of your soul to seek deeply for the living water of Jesus Christ. Again, in time, you will feel the rush of strength and fresh growth. This time it will be with renewed passion and vigor. What the enemy has tried to use for your destruction through this silent valley of doubt, God will use to turn your dark church into a temple ablaze with his honor and glory (see Ps. 71:20–21; Isa. 40:28–31; 1 Peter 5:6–10).

First Aid Tool

If you can't hear God's voice in your faithquake, watch carefully for his actions. As the adage says, they speak louder than words.

6

The Issue of Healing

His disciples asked him, "Rabbi, who sinned, this man
or his parents, that he was born blind?"

"Neither this man nor his parents sinned," said Jesus,
"but this happened so that the work of God might be displayed in his life."

John 9:2–3

Three years into our faithquake we had a one-year-old
daughter with AIDS. I was ministering as a youth pastor in Lakewood, Colorado, and up to that point, we
hadn't told anyone except our senior pastor. Ashli was
becoming visibly sick, though, and the time came to let
people know why. The pastor shared our situation with
our congregation.

The response we received was mixed. On one hand,
we received cards and letters bearing compassion and
prayers. Media sought out our story, and Evon and Ashli
appeared in the *Denver Post,* on local and national radio

programs, and on the *700 Club*. On the other hand, we also heard from people with less-than-helpful solutions.

One weekday afternoon, I heard the front door slam behind her as Evon walked into our living room with a handful of letters. Her face was red and her eyes flashed fire as she read a letter. She read quickly, then crumpled the letter and threw it on the pile with the other junk mail. As she walked past me, she summed it up in one word. "Idiots," she said.

Thinking that might be a harsh judgment, I read the crumpled letter.

She was right.

Magical Methods

Another well-meaning person had written suggesting reasons why our family had been afflicted and hadn't yet experienced healing. "Evon may be under a generational curse," one offered. Another asked, "Are you sure there is no unconfessed sin? That will prevent the Lord from healing Evon, you know."

Many had ideas that would supposedly force God's healing hand. We received "anointed" prayer cloths. Pamphlets arrived announcing the wonders of garlic and ozone treatments, and elixirs made of rose hips and other nasty ingredients. We were told to forsake medicine and consume herbs. We even slept with a Bible under our pillows. Tapes revealing more magical treatments came by the dozens.

I have to admit, we tried them all. Naive, you say? Come on, when your wife's life is at stake, you will do *anything* to see her live. When people said, "You just have to have enough faith," I took it as a personal challenge.

Eventually, though, this concept really perplexed me. We felt immense confusion every time we jumped through a hoop, full of hope and belief that God could heal Evon, but then he didn't. Like other frustrated believers, we asked, "What are we doing wrong?"

After jumping through every likely and unlikely hoop, we reached a point of surrender. We finally put away the prayer cloths and dumped the garlic. We didn't cease praying for healing, *but we let go of all the tricks we'd been using to get God's attention.* We realized we had been putting our faith in those methods rather than in God's mercy—we were seeking God only for what he could give us, not for him. The Holy Spirit alerted us that this was out of order. Evon once asked me pointedly, "Isn't it amazing that we spend more time on the healing than we do with the Healer?"

After some time and study, I concluded that there are a few things we *know:* God is a merciful and healing God. He loves each one of us. Sickness is not in his design for humankind—it entered the world only after humans chose a path contrary to God's. But not everyone will be healed, and many of the doctrines we manipulate from these truths can be hazardous to those in pain. Let me show you how I reached my conclusions.

What God Requires

Let's look at some scriptural accounts and see how much faith is really required for healing.

In John 9:1–12, the disciples apparently shared the popular notion that unconfessed sin resulted in physical disease. Jesus made clear that the man born blind was not under a generational curse, nor was his sin a factor. Actually Jesus revealed, "This happened so that the work of God might be displayed in his life" (v. 3). And it was—Jesus' healing of this man created quite a stir in the city. It opened the door for Jesus to preach about himself as the Good Shepherd.

The healing of the man at the pool of Bethesda (John 5:1–15) is startling in its implications. John describes the pool where "a great number of disabled people used to lie" (v. 3). Yet when Jesus walked by, he healed only the older man who had been there for thirty-eight years. Evidently Jesus walked by many sick and crippled people but did not stop to heal them. What did the man who was healed do that the others didn't? Is there a method to be learned here? No. It was simply an act of God's great mercy on the man.

Remember the story of Peter and John healing the beggar at the temple gate in Acts 3:1–10? Luke writes, "A man crippled from birth was being carried to the temple gate called Beautiful, where he was put *every day* to beg from those going into the temple courts" (v. 2, emphasis mine). Jesus must have seen him in the three years previous to his healing. Again here is a sick man whom Jesus didn't heal.

In another setting, Capernaum this time, Jesus was preaching when four men lowered their paralyzed friend to Jesus through a hole in the roof (Mark 2:1–12). When Jesus saw their faith, he said to the paralytic, "Son, your sins are forgiven" (v. 5). The man hadn't even made a confession! Was he healed? Not yet. Moments later, Jesus went one step further and healed him to testify to the teachers of the law that he could forgive *and* heal. Again the man himself didn't seem to display any great show of faith. (In fact it was the faith of the man's *friends* that prompted Jesus to forgive him his sins and ultimately heal him! Another case of God cramping our theological box.) We can wring no method from this account. Again it is an example of God's mercy.

This is why Evon and I finally decided to rest in God's mercy. We could see from Scripture that God's decision to heal wasn't dependent on the actions or performance of the afflicted. It depends on his choice and his plan. And no matter what he decides, we are awash in his mercy. We had come to grips with two truths. First, God truly loved us and had done everything to provide *eternal* healing, life, and happiness for us. Second, our physical life is, by nature, temporal and limited. Dying is entering a doorway into a greater—and perfect—dimension of life and existence. It is not the end.

Finally grasping these truths gave us a new perspective on healing. While we continued asking for it, we rested our lives in the hands of the merciful God who would hold us close unto death—and beyond. His mercy is unchanging.

What does God require for healing? James 5:14–15 offers the only instruction available, and it's blessedly simple. "Is any one of you sick?" he writes. "He should call the elders of the church to pray over him and anoint him with oil in the name of the Lord. And the prayer offered in faith will make the sick person well; the Lord will raise him up. If he has sinned, he will be forgiven."

First Aid Tool — When seeking healing, stick to scriptural, not human, mandates.

We can see that Scripture negates the methodology promoted in many churches today. All of the hoops that modern healing evangelists ask us to jump through mean nothing. God can and does heal today, but his healing is an act of sheer mercy. It is the exception, not the rule, that people get healed. We should rejoice for those who receive this blessing from God and not find ourselves envious or covetous. You see, God sees the big picture. We don't. His intervention into human sickness, whether by healing or by maintaining our spiritual health in the midst of not healing, is always merciful.

This may seem cold and abrasive to you who deeply hunger for God's healing touch. You know that God desires to heal spiritually—giving you eternal life. We also know that this is of greater value than a physical remedy, since everyone who gets healed also eventually dies. Looking deeply into the heart of God, we learned, we can find comfort in the fact that God's love never changes.

What do you do to get healed? Just pray and obey. Do what God says to do. If you follow the biblical mandates and don't get healed, don't fret. Don't assume you lacked enough faith. God has chosen a different path for you. Remember, Jesus went to prepare a place for us (John 14:2–3). That place is not here.

Dictating to God

Dear Job,

I can't wait until I walk the streets of gold. What a day that will be. I want desperately to meet you. I would like to see your entire family. I especially want to discuss perspectives of life with your children who died in the storm. I would also like to talk about thankfulness with the children that God gave you after the storm. But most of all, I'd like to give you a big hug and just talk.

Sincerely,
Doug Herman

P.S. I too have tried to dictate to God.

Have you ever heard anyone try to dictate to God how he should behave and act? Sure. We all have, to some degree or another. Even in the Garden of Gethsemane, Jesus asked for another way. But finally he yielded his will to that of his Father.

I love to preach a sermon called "the Book of Job." That's right, the entire book. I have trouble cutting up this book and preaching only parts of it. The context gives such vital balance to any individual verse that to preach only about the "wager" between God and Satan or Job's friends is like telling a half-truth. (If you haven't read the Book of Job, I highly recommend it. He was a very human example of someone enduring a faithquake.)

This book is particularly instructional in terms of showing us the things we *shouldn't* do. In reading, we find that Job was absolutely righteous. That is, he didn't do anything wrong. And we see that God allowed tremendous adversity and pain in Job's life. We see the reactions of Job, his wife, and his friends. We hear chapter upon chapter of Job and his friends trying to figure out why. We finally hear Job unleash his hurt to God and demand a face-to-face meeting to confirm his innocence.

First Aid Tool

Real faith doesn't make demands of God. It leaves the choice to him.

In the last five chapters, we find Job cowering in fear as God preaches the greatest sermon recorded in Scripture of his own power and glory. In summary, he proves again and again that man's power and knowledge are woefully inadequate next to that of the Almighty. Job agrees and states, "Surely I spoke of things I did not understand, things too wonderful for me to know. . . . I despise myself and repent in dust and ashes" (42:3, 6).

Job had tried to tell God how to run the universe. He thought quite highly of himself; that is, until he met God.

We can learn much from Job. Contrary to what many pastors and well-meaning believers state, we have no right to hold God to a "contract" of perfect health and happiness. For one thing, it's a promise he never made. For another, we stand in arrogance when we demand anything of God. As we can see from Job's example, such an attitude is unwise and promises to be severely humbling. God *always* has the last word.

It's important to note that even in Job's intense suffering, God proved merciful. He sent friends, who were at first a consolation (remember how they sat with him for seven days—Job 2:13). He didn't forsake Job, even when Job vented his anger. He brought the suffering to an end and restored Job's family and fortunes.

An evangelist from Ghana shared with me his perspectives of life and suffering. Having observed American Christianity and those who try to dictate to God, he made a statement that has stuck with me to this day. "You Americans have it all wrong. It is not 'Master, do this. Master, do that,'" he said. "It is 'Yes, Master. Whatever you say, Master. I'm *yours*, Master.'"

This is hard theology for Americans to swallow. Maybe it is because our nation is built upon our rebellion from authority. But in Christianity, it is accurate and ultimately inescapable.

Presumptuous Faith

We could call this dictatorial attitude toward our maker "presumptuous faith"—faith that presumes certain things are a given. In my life I would exercise this type of "faith" as well.

In 1986 and 1987 I attended several conferences for youth pastors and ministers. People were preaching a lot then about being a risk taker for God. We were to step out in faith and see what would happen. "Put yourself into a position where God would have to respond," we were instructed. This seemed to be the daring, reckless faith the Bible called for. Eventually I put myself into just such a position.

Before I tell you more of my story, let me explain that knowing that my wife was HIV-positive did not mean to me that she was actually carrying the AIDS virus. I knew a blood test reflecting an HIV-positive status meant Evon had been exposed to the virus that causes AIDS—but that didn't mean to me that it would necessarily, absolutely escalate into full-blown AIDS. God could intervene at any time. In fact at one point my "faith" (some would call it *denial*) was such that I no longer believed Evon was even carrying the HIV. I truly believed that God had removed the infectious virus and that her immune system would simply register a positive HIV test until it flushed itself clean from these antibodies in a few years.

However, with this perspective, I felt I needed to prove my faith to God. I wanted to show him I was not living in fear. Our marriage had become burdened by protective measures, and I began to see those as signs of fear, signs of doubt that God had healed my wife. After all, he had protected me for the eighteen months before we learned of the HIV; surely that was evidence. I decided it was time to step out in faith and let God be God.

In late January of 1988, my wife and I had a wonderful evening of intimacy. In the passion of the evening, without telling Evon, I allowed our intercourse to be unprotected. While an exhilarating experience, it was also alarming. Evon feared for my safety. We wondered about pregnancy. Yet we still held to the belief that we were stepping out in true faith—putting ourselves in a position of ultimate trust and risk. The statement echoed in my mind: *Put yourself into a position where God would have to respond.* "Well, God," I said, "it is your turn now." Two months later, we learned Evon was pregnant.

Her pregnancy was uneventful, and she gave birth to Ashli on November 4, 1988. As I said in chapter 1, we found out that Ashli had AIDS early the next summer.

What had gone wrong? I couldn't believe it. I was shattered. Although still at risk myself, I experienced great remorse for my daughter. It was then that I went to the church at 2:00 A.M. to have that serious talk with God.

I have learned—at quite a painful expense—that we cannot dictate to God how and when he should perform for us. I have learned what faith is and what faith is not. And I know very well the dangers of presumption.

Faith is *not* putting ourselves into a position that forces God to intervene on our behalf. Nor is it trying to impress him with our great trust so that he responds in awe of our exploits. Real faith expresses itself in sure obedience and submission to God. Real faith follows his clear directives, regardless of the circumstances in which we find ourselves.

For me this meant following the Scriptures' commands to have the church pray with us for healing. We should have shared our situation with the entire congregation immediately so they could help carry our burden (Gal. 6:2). And having done all that the Bible directed, we were to rest in the assurance of God's grace and mercy. We were not to try to dictate how God should respond to us. We were not to take extreme measures of presumptuous faith. We were to pray, obey, and leave the results in God's hands.

Job should have submitted to his God, not confronted him with a haughty agenda. Job presumed he could make God admit he was wrong. I presumed that God would not allow this random tragedy to occur to us who deeply love him. I placed myself and my unborn daughter in danger by presuming that I was in control of the protective hand of God. Neither Job nor I was walking in wisdom.

For me this presumption was an unspeakable mistake. Had I known then the tragedy, pain, and suffering that would follow in its wake, I never would have considered so vain a concept. I was young, immature, and had no one to guide me to wisdom—even if anyone had, I was too proud to hear his or her voice.

I now speak often at high school assemblies on the topics of AIDS and abstinence. During the question-and-answer session following one of these, a young teacher asked a question I could not answer. In fact it brought me to tears.

"Mr. Herman, if you had to do it all over again, would you conceive Ashli a second time?"

I stood motionless as a whirlwind of emotions rushed my being. *Of course, I would never put her through that pain again,* I thought to myself. *But I'd do anything to hold her again, to feel the way she used to gently stroke my eyelashes.*

I could not answer, and I explained why.

While my regrets are deep, I have found even deeper forgiveness in my heavenly Father. I can assure you, if you have fallen as I have, what the enemy purposed for our destruction, God will use for his glory. The enemy has always desired to steal, kill, and destroy us (John 10:10). Our victory over death has secured my wife and daughter eternally in the mansions of heaven. Satan has lost the battle for their souls. He attacked my spirit with twisted doctrines, which produced nothing but confusion and guilt. He now attacks with remorse and bitterness. Yet he loses again as I see my failures through the eyes of Christ—finding understanding, forgiveness, and acceptance.

I was presumptuous, and for that I am sorry. But part of my redemption today is the fact that I have a little girl eagerly awaiting my arrival in heaven, where for the first time I will hear her call me "Daddy."

In the battles between mercy and methods, faith and presumption, submit your understanding to God's infinite wisdom. Don't try to "force" his action. Trust him with your life the way you trust him with your soul.

7

Stand Firm

Therefore put on the full armor of God, so that when the
day of evil comes, you may be able to stand your ground,
and after you have done everything, to stand.

Ephesians 6:13

Closing my truck door, I walked briskly into the office
entrance of our church. I was late again. Music was playing in the main sanctuary, and I could hear hundreds of
eager church attendees chatting amiably. Slipping into
my suit jacket as I entered the senior pastor's office, I
looked at the people gathered to pray before the early
service. I'm sure that, to them, I looked stressed and
disheveled. My pastor smiled warmly—and disarmingly.
"What's the good word this morning, Doug?" he asked
with a tinge of humor in his voice.

The good word? I thought of the events of the past two
years. *The good word? I don't have a good word! I just
want to make it through my personal valley right now. I
just want to survive.*

Every eye was fixed on me, awaiting some response. "The good word, pastor, is *stand,*" I said. "Just stand!"

They didn't seem to understand what I meant. I didn't care if they did or not. My wife and I had just discovered that our six-month-old daughter had contracted AIDS, and my wife was now battling some effects from the virus as well. No one knew of our HIV infection other than the pastor at this point. He did not know of my inner battles with the reality and silence of God. I was dry and desperate. I felt I was not going to make it through the trials that loomed before me. The good word? It's hard to find a good word when you feel as if all is hopeless.

What It Means to Stand

In my high school assemblies about AIDS and abstinence, I always tell my own story. Having just shaken the students with that, I usually receive a wide variety of questions.

One particular afternoon, a long-haired young man wearing a heavy-metal T-shirt raised his hand. "Yeah, man. Like, uh, that's pretty intense! But didn't you, like, think of getting out? I mean, dude! I'd be, like, thinking of killing myself or something if that happened to me. Did you ever think about that? How'd you make it?"

His honesty impressed me, and I instantly respected him. With all the compassion and strength of my soul, I began to explain that both Evon and I had those thoughts. At times we did want to quit. I even envisioned putting my entire family in our running car and closing the garage door behind us to die by carbon-monoxide poisoning. "But think about this from my son's point of view," I said. "Don't you think that's awfully selfish? Besides, as painful as it was, I have never been one to quit. My father taught me that quitting is for the weak. That is one of the reasons I am here. No matter what you go through, you can make it."

The student nodded and sat down. I wondered if he really grasped the truth that we *can* stand through life's toughest trials.

Quitting seems all too common today. Look at the divorce and suicide rates. Obviously many people are not content with their lives. The actions range from drastic to insignificant, but they are indicative of people who do not follow through. And tempting though it was to give it all up during our faithquake, Evon and I decided instead to stand. For us that meant enduring the thoughtless reactions of people. It meant we would continually seek medications and treatments in conjunction with our prayers for healing. We had decided to stand in our faith, continuing to seek God and worship him as Lord even though we didn't understand him. We could easily have given up, and though we were greatly tempted at times to do so, we stood instead.

First Aid Tool

When the ground is shaking the most, keep standing. Never, ever give up spiritual ground.

Above all, in our efforts to stand, we had to fight another enormous temptation: spiritual anemia.

Another Deadly Disease

Anemia is a condition of the blood where a deficiency of hemoglobin accompanied by reduced red blood cell counts causes weakness and breathlessness. Anemia is expressed physically in decreased power, vigor, and vitality.

Spiritual anemia has parallel symptoms. They are even more serious than the physical ones because they are soul-deep—of eternal significance. The spiritually anemic person lacks the power, enthusiasm, and heartiness of soul required not only to endure a faithquake but to rebuild after having one.

I have experienced both extremes spiritually—times when I've been used of God in amazing ways and have felt so close to him and times when, as I've described, I could hardly find him. The second circumstance, common to faithquake victims, provides the most difficult time to choose to stand.

See if you relate to this story.

On our high school football team we had an offensive tackle named Don. Don was very large and very strong. But he was not known for his mental quickness or physical agility. In one particular game, Don was receiving a beating from the defense of a Catholic high school. Play after play they targeted the strength of our line. We began to see the beatings take their toll as Don slowly dragged himself back to the huddle. Soon Don lost all concern about the game, letting the defense blast through the line, punishing our backs.

Having had his fill of pain for the day, Don lumbered back to our huddle and numbly announced, "I don't want to play anymore."

Joe, our fullback and the meanest guy on the team, shouted back to Don, "Then get off the team!"

"Okay," Don said, and he began to saunter to the sidelines.

Our coach saw him leaving and shouted back, "Don! Get back in there and block!"

"Okay" was all he could say as he turned and began to drag his feet back to the huddle.

"Get off the field!" we shouted back to Don. He would turn back to the sidelines only to hear the coach again shout, "Don, get in there and block!"

Have you ever felt like Don, that you had no real alternatives? On the one hand, you have your personal disaster. It's terrifying. It's overwhelming. It's impossible. On the other hand, you have quitting—running away from the situation by getting high or getting out. I've felt the tug of war. Now is the most critical time to stand. It is time to become the overcomers God has made us.

The Blood of an Overcomer

Dr. Paul Brand and Philip Yancey collaborated to write a book entitled *In His Image*. In it they describe a situation that illuminates the concept of overcoming.

> Some years ago an epidemic of measles struck Vellore and one of my daughters had a severe attack. We knew she would recover, but our other infant daughter, Estelle, was dangerously vulnerable because of her age. When the pediatrician explained our need for convalescent serum, word went around Vellore that the Brands needed the "blood of an overcomer." We did not actually use those words, but we called for someone who had contracted measles and had overcome it. Serum from such a person would protect our little girl.
>
> It was no use finding somebody who had conquered chicken pox or had recovered from a broken leg. Such people, albeit healthy, could not give the specific help we needed to overcome measles. We needed someone who had experienced measles and had defeated that disease. We located such a person, withdrew some of his blood, let the cells settle out, and injected the convalescent serum. Equipped with "borrowed" antibodies, our daughter fought off the disease successfully. The serum gave her body enough time to manufacture her own antibodies. She overcame measles not by her own resistance

or vitality, but as a result of a battle that had taken place previously within someone else.[1]

What a contrast to the condition brought on by anemia! A person with "overcoming" blood has developed defense mechanisms ready to abolish invading disease. Rather than being weak and without vigor, this person's blood is powerful and zealous to defend.

If, in the face of crisis, you and I are anemic in the spiritual sense, we need a transfusion. This must come from one who has already encountered the disease of sin and subdued it. We need the blood of an overcomer—Jesus Christ.

When God came to earth in the form of man, it was not simply to give us wonderful holidays where we can decorate trees and celebrate beautiful sunrises. While I enjoy Christmas and Easter tremendously, I know that God entered our world to endure the full brunt of sin's fury and overcome it. As Brand and Yancey state,

> It is as if He went out of His way to expose Himself to temptation, to encounter the stress and strain you and I will meet—to gain wise [overcoming] blood for our benefit. Beginning with His personal struggle with Satan in the wilderness, Jesus declined to use naked power to overcome temptations toward success, power, and an escape from the limitation of humanity. In the Garden of Gethsemane those temptations put Him to the ultimate test, but "for the joy set before him [He] endured the cross, scorning its shame" (Heb. 12:2).[2]

God came to earth in the form of man so that we could overcome evil—including the temptation to quit—and the diseased attacks of sin in our lives. The only way possible for us to succeed against sin—to stand—is to accept the blood of one who has already overcome. The writer of Hebrews reminds us, "We do not have a high priest who is unable to sympathize with our weaknesses, but we have one who has been tempted in every way, just as we are—yet was without sin" (4:15). John writes about the key to defeating sin's author, Satan, in Revelation 12:11: "They *overcame* him by the blood of the Lamb and by the word of their testimony" (emphasis mine). That same power is available to you and me.

First Aid Tool Don't be afraid to admit yourself for frequent "transfusions"—your weakness for his strength.

We talked about our calling as disciples in chapter 3, the fact that "Christ suffered for you, leaving you an example, that you should follow in his steps" (1 Peter 2:21). We're all familiar with the "Footprints" poem in which the author suggests that on the tough roads in life, there is only one set of footprints because at that point Jesus carries us. I propose another reason: There is only one set of footprints because that is when we finally realize that we cannot endure hardship in our own strength. Therefore, we must follow in the steps of one who has previously overcome.

A Final Note on Standing

Many of us keep energized in our "stand" in faith through the use of spiritual warfare tactics. In a faithquake, though, new issues present themselves. How do you practice spiritual warfare—binding spirits, praying down strongholds, rebuking the enemy with the Word of God—in the context of God-allowed suffering? To whom do you quote the Word of God? Whose hand do you rebuke? We know that when the enemy comes against us, we stand in the assurance of the blood of Christ and rebuke his attack in the name of Jesus. But when suffering comes by the permission of the hand of God, what then?

We have already established that suffering is common, and God often uses this process to refine his creations and prepare them to comfort one another. We know from Scripture that the spiritual battle is the Lord's (as David discovered in 1 Sam. 17:47), yet we are also called to swing the sword and wear the armor. Paul mentions this specifically: "Therefore put on the full armor of God, so that when the day of evil comes, you may be able to stand your ground, and *after you have done everything, to stand*" (Eph. 6:13, emphasis mine).

I certainly tried to do everything I could in the realm of spiritual warfare. I had prayed, fasted, stepped out in faith, spoken positively, confessed healing, had my wife anointed with oil, received prayer cloths, had my family listen to Scripture healing tapes, attended a national healing crusade, even slept with a Bible under my pillow! I had done *everything* I could think of, spiritually speaking, yet found no relief. I couldn't rebuke God for allowing AIDS to invade our lives. I couldn't pray down his strongholds. What then?

Paul said to put on the armor so that "after you have done everything" you'll be able "to stand." I remember discovering the ability to do this. It wasn't in a book, a sermon, or a friendly conversation. It involved acts of spiritual warfare, to be sure, but not the usual kind. These actions were *toward* someone—God—not *against* someone—Satan. This discovery was forged on the anvil of pain as I found myself broken time and time again under the harshness of life and the power of God's presence. I gained the ability to stand through the spiritual tactics of weeping, worship, and absorbing the Word.

Weeping reveals a broken and contrite heart before God. I could not allow the enemy to destroy me from the inside out, so I had to choose against becoming hard-hearted and scornful of God's choices. Allowing myself to weep openly during the painful moments in life was liberating. It helped me release all the pent-up anger, sorrow, and frustration that threatened to overwhelm my faith.

Worship, that tender expression of love between us and our heavenly Father, also galvanized my ability to stand. Acknowledging his attributes in the midst of suffering kept me pliable before him. I looked to him as my only source of joy and comfort. I refused to look to the world and sin for its temporary comforts as I knew this was another of the enemy's snares.

The Word, I found, could no longer be a decorative book placed behind my desk or on our coffee table. The Word of God had to become something real and alive. It had to become active and effective. In my efforts to learn to stand, I didn't just read the Word, but I memorized paragraphs and meditated upon them for weeks and even months. For example, I memorized and meditated on James 1:2–4 for about six months. I learned more about true joy and the processes of God in that time than any seminary ever could have taught me.

The three *W*s became my new tools for spiritual warfare. They kept me mindful of who the enemy really was and how best I could undermine his energy in my life.

Don't Just Stand There—Stand Firm!

Remember the blow-up clown punching bag we played with as children? For me it was more than a plaything—it was a personal challenge. I remember the hours of joy that turned to frustration as I tried to overcome this foe. It seemed that every time I landed a good hit on his nose, up he'd pop again. With a smile! He kept standing and standing. Again and again I would hit him, even jump on him. He kept smiling and standing. The pound or two of sand at his base would act as an anchor, holding his "feet" to the ground. This foundation was greater than any blow that came his way. Regardless of the intensity of the assault, he would eventually rise again due to the mass and weight of his foundation.

Our foundation is Jesus Christ. He is greater than any circumstance that comes to destroy us. Regardless of the intensity of the assault, we too will rise again. Let your confidence swell with the new revelation that we truly are "more than conquerors through him who loved us" (Rom. 8:37).

We too are to stand tall. Even when we experience the power of adversity and pain, we can stand again. Just like the clown with a permanent smile, we can receive all the attacks that hell can muster. When we are down and have done everything we know to do, our job is simply to stand. Allow the overcoming blood of Christ to be your source of strength and stand firm. (And if you want to really get under the devil's skin while you're standing—smile.)

Part 2

REBUILDING
TOOLS

8

Rebuilding after Faithquake

From the depths of the earth
you will again bring me up.

Psalm 71:20

"Daddy, where are we going?" Joshua asked nervously. He was about to be enrolled in kindergarten. First, he needed his inoculations. By this time we had lived in Colorado for two years. Little Ashli was nineteen months old, and both she and Evon were increasingly ill. Joshua loved to ride along with me in my truck, but today he knew something was different.

At four years of age, Joshua was quite perceptive. On this particular day, he noticed that we were not headed to the mall or the church. Instead, we were driving by large office buildings and complexes. To him this was intriguing, confusing, and nerve-racking, because they looked *a lot* like the buildings where the doctor's office was. Since Mommy and Ashli were not in the truck, that meant only one thing: *He* was the patient. And to him being the patient meant needles, pain, and lots of crying.

With a hint of fear, he again asked, "Daddy, where are we going?"

I tried to be casual. "We're going to the doctor's office, Josh."

"B-but why? Why are we going to the doctor's office?"

I didn't want to tell him the whole truth. You parents may understand my dilemma. How do you break the news to an inquisitive child that pain is in his imminent future? I thought I might fake him out with a complex-sounding answer. "You need an inoculation, Josh."

"What's an inoculation?" The fear was not gone.

I was trying to be creative. *Think, Doug!* What is an inoculation? *Don't scare him. Don't lie. Be creative. Think! You can do it.*

"Uh . . . that's a shot, Josh." *Wow. What brilliance.*

I guessed his response correctly. Tears flowed freely as Josh scooted his bottom into a protective posture against the passenger door. "I don't want a shot, Daddy. I don't *want* a shot."

I tried ineptly to explain the necessity of inoculation. "Josh, they are going to give you an inactive form of a bacteria. It will go into your body and build up anti-bodies. . . ." Right over his head. He couldn't get past the needle.

Josh continued to assert his right to protest. Our conversation lasted all the way into the doctor's office. "I'm not sick. I don't need a shot, Daddy. You love me, don't you? Please, Daddy. I don't want a shot!"

At the office the doctor prepared the needle, and we turned Josh facedown on the padded examination table. "It's going to be all right," I reassured him. His whimpering crescendoed into a full cry.

I don't know who was more tense, Josh, me, the nurse, or the doctor. It took three of us to keep him on the table.

The nurse pinned his arms down, I held his head steady. Doctor Meyer leaned over his kicking legs and bared Joshua's backside. In one quick movement, he administered the shot.

When they stuck him with the needle, Josh looked straight at me. Looking deep into my eyes as I firmly held his head, he cried "Daddy!" It was only one word, but his look said a million words. "Daddy, why the pain? Ouch, Daddy! Why are you letting them hurt me? I thought you were my father! It's not my fault. Why, Daddy? I thought you loved me."

Josh's face reflected pain. It showed fear. But he also had a startling look of disappointment—like I had let him down.

My eyes burned with tears as my mind suddenly raced to the familiar phrases I had uttered months before. "Why, God? I thought you loved me! I thought you were my Father! Why, Daddy? Why?"

Suddenly I heard a voice. Though not an audible voice, clearly God spoke to my heart at that moment. He simply said, "It's the same with you and me."

A new understanding of who he is flooded my heart. You see, if I could explain the full reason for the inoculation to my son, I would. I love him. I would die for him. But even if I explained it, he wouldn't grasp it. For he can only understand simple, concrete thought. Until his mind matures, he can't understand abstract thoughts such as eternity . . . inertia . . . inoculation!

So it is with our heavenly Father. While we can handle some complex thoughts, God is divine. He is *all-knowing*! His level of thought so exceeds our own that we can never fully understand the reasons why he acts as he does. Yet if he could explain all the answers to our whys, he would. Right now, the answers would go right over our heads, and we would label them "illogical." Many circumstances in life don't make sense. But that does not mean he does not love us. He does. So much so, that he would die for us . . . and did.

I picked up Josh and held him. "It's okay, Josh. Daddy loves you. I'm sorry that hurt. It's going to be okay. Daddy's here. Daddy loves you." With every word I said to Josh, I could see the tear-stained face of my Father in heaven reassuring me of his love for me. I hugged Joshua and sensed God holding me and stroking my wounded soul, whispering strength and affection into my spirit.

> **Rebuilding Tool**
>
> When you're rebuilding from senseless rubble, one stone stands true: Your Father loves you.

It was then that my faith began rebuilding. I knew I was going to make it. While there was much I did not understand, I knew my Father in heaven loved me.

The Father Heart of God

When we hear God described as a father, mental pictures flash within each of us. Some of us think of a cruel abuser. Some have no picture at all. Others visualize paternal apathy holding greater interest in the daily paper or a sports program. I, however, see a picture of extreme compassion. I think of my dad.

During my childhood, he displayed his love for me in various ways. Whether shouting his support at a wrestling match or building a business to hand to me in the future, I knew he loved me. But nothing was better than his touch—his just being there.

My fondest memories of Sunday evening church don't include how the music sounded, the many faces who attended our church, or even the sermons preached. It was the *experience*. For forty-five minutes I got to hang out with my dad, sitting on his lap and napping in his arms. The unique smell from the combination of his perspiration and Brut in our non-air-conditioned church was intriguing and reassuring rather than offensive. This was my dad. He loved me. And I loved him.

Since my dad was wonderful and compassionate, I knew God was as well. What a shock when AIDS, through no action of our own, invaded our lives, and this God suddenly seemed disinterested. That moment with my son, where God gently but vividly reminded me of his unchanging care for me, brought me back to a working faith. I re-realized that the Father's heart is a deep well of compassionate strength. It reassures us that regardless of the twists and turns in the valleys of our lives, we have a Father who knows, sees, feels, and never leaves us. And he sees the big picture.

The captain and crew of a big ship struggled desperately to maneuver their vessel through a narrow river bordered by jagged cliffs. Thick fog complicated and confused their efforts. Their destiny seemed one of certain destruction, but they survived the encounter by remaining silent and listening for the faint voice of the man standing in the crow's nest atop the main mast. From his vantage point, he could see above the fog and navigate their path between the cliffs. The captain and crew responded in total obedience to this man's directions because this man saw the big picture.

> **Rebuilding Tool**
>
> When you can't find your way, listen quietly for the Father's voice. He sees the big picture.

I too am a father. Because I see the big picture of my son's life, and because I love him, I often allow him to experience hurt and disappointment. This may not always make sense to him. Yet I know that as he overcomes these challenges he will emerge more mature, strengthened by his experience. He will be able to handle future adversity with greater grace and understanding. If you get a moment, reread the story that began this chapter. This time, read it from the perspective of a father who knows what is coming and wants to do what's best for his son. As he watches his son enjoying the ride, oblivious to the hour of pain ahead, he feels inner torment at the thought of sending him into that pain. But he sees the big picture. He knows that inoculations protect his son from crippling and deadly disease. As you read, you will see the father's heart at work.

From the child's perspective, it seems like a dirty trick, as if his father sold him out. Until the child fully understands his father's perspective, he will not understand the father's purpose. It isn't that the father does not love him. To the contrary, he loves him enough to allow temporary pain that affects his child, not to mention himself, so he can provide future health and life.

This is how God deals with us. God doesn't want us to experience any pain. He has no desire to see his children suffer. But if this temporal suffering provides a greater blessing, whether we understand it or not, he will allow it. He sees what we cannot.

I still wrestle with this today, but it is true. Because God loves us, he allows the pain.

9

When Everything You Believe Is Shaken

I have set the LORD always before me.
Because he is at my right hand,
I will not be shaken.

Psalm 16:8

King David experienced many faithquakes in his lifetime. His statement in Psalm 16:8 challenges me. In my life I have put the Lord before me. I have placed him at my right hand. But *I was shaken.*

How can we resolve the truth of God's Word and the reality of our faithquakes? Is it possible to truly "not be shaken"? I think so. Let me explain.

David wrote Psalms 15 and 16 after the ark of the covenant had been brought into Jerusalem. As you remember, David danced his praise (2 Samuel 6). This was a period of joy and establishment in Israel's Jehovah God. As David penned those psalms, he focused on the presence of God. If we abide there, he seemed to assert, we will not be shaken, because God cannot be shaken. This is true. One of the prophets, probably Ezra, reiterated this idea in Psalm 125 following Babylonian captivity. Without God as our foundation, first and foremost, we can be deeply shaken.

David and the prophet wrote of a deep truth that our emotions may or may not validate. Neither can our intellect fully grasp its meaning. This is a truth of the spirit. When we experience a shaking in life, we feel it emotionally and struggle with it intellectually. But *spiritually* we can survive intact when we live our lives in God's presence.

This is the deep, inner communion with God where spiritual truths are found and strengthened. It is here that we abide in the presence of Christ. It is here that we cannot be shaken.

Sad to say, we often allow our spiritual security to find its foundation in elements other than Christ himself. We may have all the training and heritage of Christianity, but we have never personally anchored our soul onto this immovable Rock. This was the situation I found myself in when we discovered that Evon was HIV-positive. I had been taught about Christ. I knew him as Savior and Lord but not yet as Rock. Thus I was shaken.

The Charge of Emotional Escapism

With four generations of Christian ministers in my family, I could not escape the foundations of the faith as they were taught and lived before me as a child. The Bible was such a familiar book in our home. You could always hear my mother singing hymns as she went about the house doing her unending chores. How I cherish finding my father in his study early on a Saturday evening preparing for the adult Bible class he has taught for nearly three decades. Yes, I have a strong Christian foundation, laid as deep as it is broad.

Yet even with such a foundation, there come times in our lives when all we have ever believed to be true is shaken. In the midst of deep shaking, we all question what we hold to be true. Therefore, we must find the unshakable truth and build our lives upon it.

During our faithquake, I had to deal with such charges as:

"Christianity is nothing but a crutch."

"Christianity is filled with contradictions yet promotes absolutes that damage and demean the lives of those it strives to help."

"Christianity is nothing more than emotional escapism, providing an emotional structure of beliefs that provide an escape of false hope from the realities of life until death."

I have grappled with these statements over the years, never more than when we were shuddering in our faithquake. Many of us wrestle with them in some form or another. I guess the bottom line is this: Is Christianity really *real?* If not, then everything we say and do as Christians is a joke. We purport a false doctrine and take the hearts and finances of those in need with us. We base our lives on mere fantasy, which eventually disappoints us fatally.

If, on the other hand, it *is* real, then we can build our lives and rest our souls on the strength and security it provides.

As "What do I believe?" ripped at my heart, the concept of "emotional escapism" challenged me. I wondered if my faith had all along been just an escape hatch from reality—something I used to shield myself from life's cruelties. This is not unlike the alcoholic who leans on his drink to escape the harshness of life, only to wake up with a hangover and the sobering reality of another morning. People who use religion solely as a coping mechanism slip further and further from reality. They become "so heavenly minded they are of no earthly good." Had this happened to me?

If I had been using my faith to shield myself from life's reality, it was not working. The reality of my family's battle with AIDS, my brother's battle with leukemia, and the imminent death they all faced forced me from behind this shield, and I was left with one question: What is truth?

I've described my "study in silence" and my exercises in asking God why. Now I dug down beyond doctrine to the foundation. Was God real? Would my family live? If they died, where would they go—really? I began to look in the mirror and ask myself: "Why am I a Christian?"

I realized that I had to determine if Christianity was real or not. I didn't want to read a bunch of books from other men. I wanted to find the truth on my own.

What Is Truth?

Sitting on an airplane, it's common for the person sitting beside me to ask what I do for a living. "I speak and write," I reply.

"Really! What do you write about?" they will quickly ask. Now, I know it's a setup, but God opens the door and I love walking through it. "Faith in the midst of tragedy," I respond. Rich conversation always follows.

In one conversation, I spoke with a lady who married a wonderful man, only to have him commit suicide three months later. Her faith in God was deeply fractured. "I don't know what is real," she breathed. She wanted me to answer her questions why and prove that God exists. In great compassion, I challenged her to prove God's existence herself. Only when we take the ownership of this powerful search can we truly experience the revelation of God's life in our journey. "But here's my advice," I cautioned. "Don't stop digging until you hit something solid . . . rock solid." I then encouraged her to begin with the life of Jesus, his death, and his resurrection. Why? Because that's exactly where I had to dig myself. Although my studies were a blend of passion and desperation, they were certainly Spirit-led.

As I studied, I realized that the quest for truth is one many have taken over the centuries. In the Gospel of John, Jesus said to Pilate, "You are right in saying I am a king. In fact, for this reason I was born, and for this I came into the world, to testify to the truth. Everyone on the side of truth listens to me" (18:37). Pilate then asked, "What is truth?" He didn't wait for an answer.

Jesus' statement in John's Gospel is profound. Here we find a key in our search for truth. If Jesus was only a teacher and prophet, but not God, he was a liar (see John 10). Our faith hinges on whether that one claim is true, because all Jesus' other claims were based on it. So I knew I must determine if he is God or not.

My studies drew me to the resurrection. If I could prove that Jesus is dead, then he is not God and all Christianity is false. If I could prove he is alive, that he conquered death as Christians believe, then all that he said is true and he is God. So I began to study.

If we can prove that Christ is dead, then we can shut Christianity down today. Televangelists and Christian organizations will have to close their doors or admit their hollow teachings. So to the skeptic, this is a great challenge. I offer it to you as well. Your answers will fortify you during your faithquake and help you rebuild.

Theories of the Tomb

One of the theories offered by those who reject the resurrection of Jesus is the "swooning" theory. Proponents of this concept believe that Jesus never died on the cross, but reached such a state of unconsciousness that he appeared dead. After being placed into a damp, cool tomb, he regained consciousness and escaped.

To accept this theory is to ignore what we know about the Roman military system and its process of crucifixion. First, Jesus had received enough beatings and punishment prior to the cross that he should have been released due to his near-death physical condition—he'd paid his "penance." Second, these soldiers were not novices at the art of killing. They were trained professionals who had crucified hundreds. They made no mistakes. When the soldier tried to hurry the crucifixion by breaking the thieves' legs, he noticed that Christ was already dead. This was confirmed as he put the spear into Jesus' side, releasing the flow of blood and water that had accumulated around the heart and lungs at the point of death. Jesus had not "swooned."

Even if Jesus hadn't died but merely had been unconscious, how is a man who had been severely beaten, dehydrated, exhausted, and crucified with spikes driven through his hands and feet supposed to awaken himself in a dark tomb and unwind himself from grave clothes? (It should be noted that grave clothes were wrapped tightly and weighted with spices.) Even so, once released from the clothes, could he possibly move the enormous stone at the front of the tomb with his bleeding, bruised body and pierced hands? This endeavor would require breaking the Roman seal and fighting the trained guards armed and prepared for intruders, then walking seven miles to Emmaus and back on shattered feet. This is harder to believe than a resurrection! Jesus did not simply pass out or fall into a comatose state. He died.

Another theory suggests that Jesus died and the disciples stole the body. These same disciples, however, had scattered in panic from the guards at Gethsemane just days before (one running without his clothes). According to this theory, these fishermen and tax collectors, untrained men, had allegedly overtaken this guard station and knocked out every guard without killing him. I don't think so. It was the guards and high priests themselves who had purported this notion. No, even the guards and high priests knew better. They would have to stretch this lie awfully far to make it believable.

Some have said that the empty tomb represents a case of "mistaken identity." This theory states that Jesus died but was misplaced. When followers of Christ placed the body of Jesus into the tomb, it was dark and people were in a hurry. They unknowingly placed him in the wrong tomb. Upon the return of the women to anoint Jesus' body again, they went to the correct tomb and found no body. Thus, the resurrection theory. (Note also, though, that the women did find grave clothes.)

This theory is completely illogical. Joseph of Arimathea, who donated his tomb to Jesus, was a rich man. He was personally with the disciples when they placed Jesus in the tomb. Could he not find his own property? This is not an easy mistake, because this was a private cemetery used by the wealthier class. It would be difficult to confuse your tomb with someone else's tomb.

The conclusion seems obvious. A final challenge to all of the tomb theories rests in a look at the history in that region following Jesus' resurrection. With rumors of this event circulating wildly, the religious officials and political leaders were feeling pressure from the followers of Christ. It was then they were named "Christians." The hatred possessed by those leaders toward the Christians was so great that intense persecution soon followed. Nero hated the Christians so much that he blamed the burning of Rome on them. All this commotion, hatred, and violence could have easily been eradicated and established the religious leaders as supreme; the political leadership could have restored peace and Roman supremacy as well. How? By simply going to the tomb and fastening the lifeless, rotting body of Jesus to a stick and parading it through the streets. "Here is your risen Christ!"

Such an action would have brought Christianity to its knees in one fell swoop. But it didn't. It couldn't. There was no body! And they knew it.

When in the course of my studies I had to conclude that Christ was real—he had risen—it secured the intellectual drive I have for God. No longer was I simply feelings-oriented, in love with God, but I was also in complete intellectual assent with what he says. I knew the Father's heart. I knew the truth. And I could stand on it—it would truly not be shaken no matter how intense the faithquake.

My Anchor Holds

Tho' the angry surges roll on my tempest-
    driven soul,
I am peaceful, for I know, wildly tho' the winds
    may blow,
I've an anchor safe and sure, that can ever-
    more endure.

Mighty tides about me sweep, perils lurk
    within the deep;
Angry clouds o'er-shade the sky, and the tem-
    pest rises high.
Still I stand the tempest's shock, for my anchor
    grips the Rock.

I can feel the anchor fast as I meet each sudden blast,
And the cable, tho' unseen, bears the heavy
strain between.
Thro' the storm I safely ride, till the turning of
the tide.

Troubles almost 'whelm the soul; griefs like
billows o'er me roll;
Tempters seek to lure astray; storms obscure
the light of day.
But in Christ I can be bold; I've an anchor that
shall hold.

And it holds, my anchor holds;
Blow your wildest then, O gale,
On my bark so small and frail.
By His grace I shall not fail, for my anchor
holds, my anchor holds.[1]

10

The Holy Use of Anger

God cannot be tempted by evil, nor does he tempt anyone; but each one is tempted when, by his own evil
desire, he is dragged away and enticed. Then, after desire
has conceived, it gives birth to sin; and sin, when it is
full-grown, gives birth to death.

James 1:13–15

One Wednesday night, Evon and I stood helpless as doctors and nurses raced our little girl to the ICU. We had
arrived at the hospital just moments earlier, and Evon
was anxious to see her daughter. Due to their concur-
rent illnesses, it had been over a week since she had held
her baby. On this evening filled with anticipation, our
hearts were crushed as Ashli experienced respiratory
alert and had to be raced to the ICU and put on a breathing machine. This was the only way they could stabilize
her heart rate and bring her oxygen levels back into a
normal range.

I escorted my weakened wife to the second floor, and we located the nurse attending our child. She instructed us on the precautions we'd have to take for Ashli's sake—wearing sterile gowns, masks, and latex gloves to protect her from our germs. Though I felt as if my world had been sucked away from me, I forced myself to remain strong for Evon, and we walked into Ashli's room together. An hour later Evon was exhausted and needed to rest in the waiting room with other friends who were there. I then had a few moments alone with Ashli.

As I looked down at her again, my strength faded into pain. Only two years old, Ashli was locked in a sterilized, glass-encased room. Naked and limp, she lay lifeless on the bed. Only the mechanized rise and fall of her chest synchronized with the beeping machine measuring her heart rate assured me that she was still alive.

Tubes and wires were strung everywhere. A urine catheter disposed of waste, a J-tube inserted into her abdomen provided nourishment, and a Broviac catheter inserted near her heart pumped life-saving medication. Cut-down lines transmitting additional medications were inserted into both wrists and one ankle. Wires from the heart monitors draped across her tiny chest, and the oxygen monitor grasped her left index finger. Her face was stretched grotesquely from the tape that held the respirator tube inserted through her mouth. Her eyes, half open and glazed from the abundance of medication, cocked strangely upward and to one side. Seemingly strangled by medical equipment, Ashli looked so tragic.

Leaning on her bed, I began to weep. *I'm sorry, God,* I thought, *but this just doesn't make sense!* I cried quietly. As I wept, a deep emotion began to erupt within me. Like a dark storm overtaking a spring day, I sensed a powerful surge. Anger began to rage like a fire, looking for someone to consume.

Looking at Ashli, I focused my anger upon the ailment that held my baby captive. I began to deeply hate AIDS and the HIV virus that causes it. AIDS doesn't care if you are two years old—or fourteen, forty, or eighty. AIDS doesn't care what city you live in or what status you hold in your community. AIDS doesn't care what color you are or how you contracted it. AIDS doesn't even care what religious background you have or what church you attend. It is merciless against the human body and spirit. I began to hate this virus with a vengeful passion.

I looked at Ashli and made a vow: *I will do whatever I can to keep this virus from attacking other children, families, and teenagers.* I promised her that her pain would not go unchampioned.

As I stared at Ashli, contemplating my vow, I found my anger unfulfilled. It was enormous and hungry. I realized that anger could use me—destroying me in the process—or I could use it and maybe accomplish something good from all this heartache. Anger requires a lot of energy—I

Rebuilding Tool

Use anger.
Don't let it use you.

could feel the way it swept me at that moment by Ashli's bedside—and I knew even then that I would need that energy for other things: For rebuilding my life after this faithquake and, as I'd vowed, for educating others about the fatal danger AIDS brings.

Where It All Begins

There in that ICU another eruption of hatred exploded within my heart. I began to think of all the suffering experienced by my wife and daughter. The countless stories of tragic pain that I had heard from other people raced through my mind. These all occurred not because God is cruel or abusive but because we have allowed sin to run rampant in our world. This sin was brought to us by Satan. He is the cause.

We know that Satan is the ultimate source of our pain. He designs blueprints on how we can be destroyed. In the second letter to the Corinthians, the apostle Paul gave instruction on reconciling a brother who had sinned and been disciplined. Paul makes his recommendations "in order that Satan might not outwit us. For we are not unaware of his schemes" (2 Cor. 2:11). Satan is scheming to destroy you today. In the middle of a faithquake, anger is a powerful tool.

Anger, you see, kills from the inside out. It is a cancer that eats away at the heart of man, leaving him hollow—void of compassion yet tainted with bitterness.

To learn how to manage this powerful force, which resides in many undergoing faithquake, we must examine anger the way God does. In Scripture we find that anger produces fruit. However, none of the fruit is beneficial. Anger stirs up dissension (Prov. 29:22) and produces strife (Prov. 30:33). When directed at a brother, it draws judgment on its sender (Matt. 5:22).

Is it wrong, then, to discover the deep rumble of anger erupting in our souls? No, no more wrong than it is for us to experience temptation. It is what we do with this eruption that is important. God himself feels anger (Ps. 95:10), so it's clearly not sinful to *feel* it. Ephesians 4:26 confirms that we can be angry yet cautions against sinning in response to it. Anger itself, in God or in us, is not sin.

So what do you do with this rising force? Proverbs 29:11 tells us, "A fool gives full vent to his anger, but a wise man keeps himself under control." We must refrain from fully venting the rage we feel at other people. Self-control, a fruit of the Spirit, is the key in handling anger.

Some of you may ask, control it *how?* Let's look at the example of Christ once again.

When God directed his anger at man, it was due to the sin and ultimate death that sin produces. God is greatly compassionate and loving toward man (Jonah 4:2). His anger finds its focus on sin, not on the sinners. We must redirect our anger in the same way, pointing it at sin but away from people and God. In doing so, we can focus our anger toward sin's author, Satan. Then we begin to destroy Satan's kingdom. How? By forgiving all, loving all, becoming humble and pliable before God, confessing our sins and weaknesses, and vowing to keep any evil from finding a foothold in our hearts. You can unload the emotional burden of anger on Satan and release the liability of sin from those who have hurt you. (They're God's business, anyway.)

This is powerfully simple and immensely necessary. We must love God, love our neighbors, and hate sin. Anything else is offensive to God. As James 1:20 says, "Man's anger does not bring about the righteous life that God desires."

Good Examples of Bad Choices

Remember in 1 Samuel when David's conquests resulted in the crowd cheering, "Saul has slain his thousands, and David his tens of thousands" (1 Sam. 18:7)? The next verse tells us, "Saul was very angry; this refrain galled him." From this point on in their relationship, Saul died inwardly. The cancer of anger ate away all that was good in him, leading to jealousy, rage, and attempted murder.

A friend I will call Lee attended the same Bible college I did. Lee was powerfully charismatic and a compelling speaker. Like all of us, though, Lee had an

Achilles heel—he openly resented any religious leadership. His sermons often contained bitterly sarcastic comments. He continued in biblical studies for a couple of years before anger won: He quit. Rage consumed his passion for ministry, and he moved away with nothing left to give in ministry. He no longer attends church at all.

Another friend, "Shane," has a story that parallels my own. After the death of his daughter, he found himself seething in anger at God. "If this is the way God is," he snarled at me, "I'll never serve him again." As you can guess, his once-vibrant faith has dwindled to nothing. He never attends church but hides behind hobbies to avoid the pain and anger within.

To all the Lees and Shanes reading this, and as one who's been there in spades, I lovingly challenge you to give up the anger you hold toward God and man. It can drain away your soul. I know how big a wall anger can create. I was furious with God for not healing Evon, Ashli, and my younger brother. I have felt immense anger toward the people of the church—nationally known preachers who

> **Focus your anger on the enemy, not on those you are called to love.**
>
> **Rebuilding Tool**

falsely promised us healing and local deacons who asked us to leave in the midst of our deepest pain. Rage boiled within me toward the gay and lesbian groups I believed promoted the spread of AIDS into a national epidemic.

But to allow this anger to dwell in my heart, I realized, was to side with Satan and his evil. I cannot focus anger upon anyone God loves. I can only love them also and turn this anger toward Satan and the sin that destroys multiple lives each day.

We tend to hold on to anger because it empowers us in a position in which we feel completely justified. We grasp it as our right. We feel we have the right to kick those who have aided or stood idly by during our faithquake. The only way I have found to release this anger is to refocus it on the one who truly works toward our destruction. This process ironically involves forgiveness and releasing your desires for vengeance. Only in this way can you find the fruit that is produced from the holy use of anger.

11

How Humor Helps

It is the heart that is not yet sure of its God that is afraid
to laugh in His presence.

George MacDonald

As the stoplight turned yellow, I glanced around for
other cars, then gunned the engine in our Astro van. Zip-
ping through the intersection, I checked my watch. *Late
again!* I rounded the corner at Bowles and Wadsworth,
headed toward Lutheran Hospital to see Evon.

Better call and let her know I'm on my way, I thought.
As I dialed Evon's room number, I pictured her there.
Was she asleep? What had her day been like? This was
her tenth prolonged stay in the hospital, and she was no
stranger to the daily routines. Being cramped in a hospital was tough for Evon; what made it even worse was
that she had lost her eyesight to retinitis ten days ago.
Evon loved the outdoors and playing with Josh in the
yard. Today was a beautiful, bright September day—I

was sure she longed to feel the sun splashing on her face, to see the glorious fall colors again. Memories of picnics and swims breezed through my mind.

Three rings, then a soft voice rasped, "Hi."

"Hi, honey. How are you doing?" I asked.

"Fine."

"I just wanted you to know I'm on my way. I'm near the Armadillo restaurant right now, headed your way. What are you doing?"

"Just sitting here in the dark, talking to you," she said, chuckling.

What was so funny? I wondered. *Oh. In the dark.* Even in such a horrible circumstance, Evon could find some humor.

"Well, don't watch too much TV," I responded. "It's bad for you." Evon laughed, and I heard her cough harshly, trying to catch her breath. "I'm sorry, Evon. You okay?"

She assured me she was fine. I hung up and continued blazing my way down the boulevard. Feelings of elation swelled within me for helping her to laugh, to have an "up" moment in that sterile, gray room.

Guilt immediately fought those feelings as I realized I had made her choke and cough, struggling for breath. The battle between emotions ended as soon as I realized what Evon would say if she could read my mind. "Doug, I would rather experience the discomfort from laughter than sit numb to life and the relationship we have."

Rebuilding Tool

Even if laughter hurts a little, it helps a lot. Use it at will.

I agreed. Sometimes when you have such a severe faithquake, you will risk some pain to experience humor, laughter, and joy, even momentarily.

Better Than Medicine

That little bit of humor is just one example of the ways Evon and I encouraged each other with laughter. Other times we found it expressed in our friends and family.

For example, Evon and her best friend, Evelyn, decided to take a class on how to make paper wreaths. Often my wife would come into the house glowing, her arms filled with bags of craft materials. Smiling, she would tell me of the class and how Evelyn couldn't get the bows to look just right—in fact they were usually so huge they were comical. Evon and Evelyn spent hours critiquing their wares and laughing until they hurt. Evelyn's friendship and availability to laugh (instead of always grieve) with Evon was powerful. In the center of her painful illness and looming death, Evon was able to reconnect with joy once again because of Evelyn. It was better than any prescription Evon's doctors could ever recommend.

Randy Smith was another friend who not only stood alongside us when our church asked us to leave, but provided the perfect dose of daily humor prior to and after our departure. For a month I awoke each morning to find a card, a prop, or a sign at my front door that joked about Randy taking my position, sitting in my big chair, and being a "big shot" like I was. All his little pranks were handmade from comics, headlines, or household items, and I still have them in a file to this day. With the termination of my ministry facing me daily, Randy was a wonderful dose of heaven-sent humor that helped me endure a trying time. His antics lightened the load and helped us find new perspective in the middle of our crisis; we were gently goaded not to take ourselves so seriously. God knew what he was doing in sending Randy, with all his creative fun, into our lives.

Evon's Aunt Ruthie was another person wonderfully gifted with a sense of humor, engaging smile, and contagious laugh. Evon called Ruthie at all hours and talked, inevitably ending up in stitches. Family is a wonderful gift, but that gift is greatly enhanced when they can help you find humor in the whirlwind of your faithquake.

Rebuilding Tool

When despair skews your perspective and chokes your joy, let your loved ones give you a double dose of humor. It won't kill you (though if you die, you'll die laughing).

Humor is a carefully crafted gift. Rather than an inappropriate response in the midst of faithquake, we found laughter liberating. We needed to find our way through the despair that surrounded us. Through friends and family too numerous to mention, we found humor to be the ultimate gift—free for the asking, more effective than medication, and a soul-saver when despair threatened to overwhelm us.

Perfect Example

To think that Jesus was a man of only somber tone is to miss the full understanding of who he is. After all, who created laughter? We can tell by the fruit. Holy, healthy laughter produces pleasure, lightens spirits, and brings relief. Since he created laughter, it is only natural to picture Jesus, God in the flesh, laughing at times with his friends. Imagine what life on the road must have been like for those twelve oddly matched disciples and you will find an abundance of great comedy.

If we examine Jesus' first miracle, changing water into wine at a wedding, we find insight into our Christ. In

The Brothers Karamazov, Dostoyevsky wrote, "Cana of Galilee.... Ah, that sweet miracle! It was not men's grief, but their joy Christ visited, He worked His first miracle to help men's gladness." Christ is greatly concerned about man's joy and gladness. And the natural expression of joy and gladness is laughter.

Some historians believe that laughter is the expression of fools. Others believe that such pleasures are forbidden for the true disciple of Christ. William Law wrote in *Christian Perfection* (1726), "The present disciples of Jesus Christ are to have no more to do with worldly enjoyments than those that He chose whilst He Himself was on earth." Some folks interpret this to mean that since the Bible records no instances of Jesus laughing, humor must be considered a "worldly enjoyment" to be avoided. How sad and how wrong! We should have no more joy than Jesus had and certainly no less. To live as one of the historical disciples who walked and lived with Jesus was to belch, scratch, and laugh like a man camping in the country during a three-year ministry tour. It is not sacrilegious to say so. Jesus Christ was fully God, fully man.

We know that Jesus wept openly. And though the Bible doesn't specifically record it, I believe he laughed openly as well. We can do the same.

Hunger for Humor

After surviving the deaths of my daughter, wife, and younger brother, I found myself suddenly drawn to comedians on television as well as to comedy materials in bookstores. I didn't understand this strange attraction. In retrospect, I think I had cried so hard for so long that I was looking for a different kind of release. Add to that the fact that I traveled nationally telling my story—

and making people cry—and I desperately wanted to be a man who could speak like the apostle Paul, "so that through my being with you again your joy in Christ Jesus will overflow on account of me" (Phil. 1:26). I was tired of the tears.

I longed to be normal again. To me normal was being able to laugh outwardly and not feel guilty for those in pain. I wanted to laugh as Evon and I had years before. But to laugh following her death seemed an offense against the memories of the pain she had endured.

Many of us have endured great pain. And many of us have found ourselves unexpectedly following those tragic moments with times of jubilation or laughter. If you too have felt the sting of guilt for enjoying life when others have died in pain, you understand my heart. But I have come to believe that to laugh is to embrace normalcy once again. It is a sign of life, similar to new green shoots of plants pressing their way through the dirt toward the sun following winter. Laughter is a tool for rebuilding. Take advantage of this gift.

Often we have friends who guide us through these rough times. Anyone with a sense of humor was a godsend to me. One December following my family's deaths, I boarded a plane for California; I was to speak to some teenagers at a large Baptist youth conference. As I entered I noticed a man whose face was familiar. It was Ken Davis, the well-known author and comedian. I saw an opportunity and I grabbed it.

"Hi!" I said. "Are you Ken Davis?"

"Yes," he said. He seemed preoccupied, but I had to press my luck.

"My name is Doug Herman. I'm speaking at the same conference in California."

"That's great," he said, trying to be polite. I knew I had to act fast if I was going to get this man to talk to me.

"Say, did you get your elk this year?" I asked, knowing his love for big-game hunting.

"Yeah! Here, sit down and I'll show you some pictures."

Ha! He was caught! I sat by him for nearly an hour looking at his many pictures of game, friends, and family. Our plane still had not taken off. Finally, someone announced over the intercom, "Ladies and gentlemen, we are having difficulties finding a crew to fly this aircraft. Our scheduled crew was illegal."

While we knew that the flight attendant meant that the crew had too many flight hours logged for their shift, that comment was all it took for a national comedian. An array of "illegal" jokes and puns poured from Ken, keeping me doubled up in laughter. Ken had no idea how I needed that, and I'm grateful to him to this day.

Laughing with people during and after the faithquakes of our lives is like sitting together in a toboggan and sliding down a steep hill. You know you may crash, but you are all facing the same way, interlocked with your legs around the rider in front of you, leaning on the pounding heart of the rider behind you, laughing and screaming at the rush of life and world as it races past you. It may not be totally safe, but it is secure.

When the End of the Rope Is Funny

Have you ever found yourself at the end of the rope, where everyone around you shakes their heads in sorrow or pity, and all you can do is burst out laughing? I have, and I can assure you that it isn't because I lost my mind. There are times when all you can say in the face of tragic circumstances is "Ha!" Of course you could curse or hit something. But at times you are so emotionally spent that all you can do is laugh. And that is a wonderful release as well.

How powerful it is to surround yourself with friends who understand this dynamic. Friends without a sense of humor can drain you even more—they don't allow you to lighten up, so everyone stays weighted down. What good is that? Those with a sense of humor can charge you with life. They give you a break, which is more than your circumstances will do. You have to find relief somewhere.

The following may not be the most spiritual example, but it is one that pulled Evon and me through some tough times. Have you seen the movie *The Money Pit?* In it Tom Hanks and Shelley Long buy a house and find that they've been swindled. Virtually nothing works, and as the hapless couple tries to rebuild and refurbish, everything short of a national disaster befalls them.

At one point, Tom Hanks's character tries to fill the bathtub for a relaxing bath. He has had all he can take; he is mentally strained and emotionally bankrupt. As he pours the water from a bucket—of course the plumbing doesn't work— the floor under the tub begins to creak. After Hanks fills the tub, it continues to creak until it cracks loose and the tub crashes through the floor to the one below—then to the one below that. Construction workers stand around in paralyzed amazement. Then Hanks begins to laugh. This is not a chuckle. It is that crazed wheeze of laughter that only those who have been stressed to the edge of insanity understand.

Rebuilding Tool

When all you can say is "Ha!" say it. Over and over, if you like.

Every time I watch this movie, that scene causes me to unroll in laughter. Not because it's a comedy and I'm supposed to laugh, but because I can relate. I am grateful for anything, especially *The Money Pit,* for helping me laugh. It's restored my equilibrium more times than I can mention. Let's face it: Sometimes all you can say is "Ha!"

Sometimes Words Won't Do

As Evon and I struggled with the imminence of her death, we found ourselves crying uncontrollably at times. One evening Evon came into my office at home and sat on my lap, leaned against my chest, and curled her legs up to her chest in a fetal position. "Honey," she cried, "I don't want to die." We wept hard together. No words would have helped.

At other times we found ourselves doubled over with laughter at silly puns, jokes, or comments. Those are the memories I cherish most. When I choose a mental picture of Evon to remember, I choose one in which we laughed so hard we cried. Laughter is truly a good medicine. Don't be afraid to use it.

12

The Battlefield of Bitterness

Each heart knows its own bitterness,
and no one else can share its joy.

Proverbs 14:10

With my wife and daughter sick with an HIV infection, we experienced many unique battles. Though I had vowed to use anger instead of letting it use me, it wasn't long before I found festering pockets of its relative—bitterness—hidden in my life. These pockets eventually became large enough to threaten all the work I had done to stand firm. Little by little, bitterness began eating away at my foundation.

While a youth pastor in a church in Denver, I told the church of our situation. The majority of the church responded with great compassion, but some were paralyzed in shock and others fled from us in fear.

Within seven days of the announcement to the church, we experienced a harsh and unexpected blow. The pastor of our church came to our house on my day off and personally explained a quarantine. The church board felt that Ashli and Evon were a health threat to pregnant moms and the elderly. He told us, "We know that 'perfect love casteth out all fear.' Doug, I'm asking you to love these people enough to remove their fears of infection. You can keep them from having to choose to reject you by pulling away from them."

Evon and Ashli were no longer allowed to use the nurseries or the kitchen. Pastors who had been very close and dear friends began to establish a distance. Their quiet rejection pierced our hearts. We didn't want to judge them for their reactions. Yet their prolonged fear and the continual fading of our friendships hurt. I learned later that the board felt we were "in denial" about how HIV is contracted—that we wouldn't be careful enough to avoid infecting others. It seemed that because we were in the youth ministry, we were somehow considered less-than-adult and not worth consulting.

We tried desperately to educate our congregation and staff with books, pamphlets, guest speakers, and access to nationally acclaimed infectious disease specialists. Regardless of our efforts, we made little progress. We began to wonder if our church family even wanted to be educated.

After nearly a year of tension and challenges, the senior pastor announced his resignation from the pulpit. As is customary in that denomination, all staff and employees tendered their resignations as well. The church board usually held the resignations for the new pastor to accept or decline. This way the new pastor had freedom to bring his own staff or utilize the present leadership.

Days after I handed my resignation to our resigning pastor, however, he visited my office and informed me that the board had accepted my resignation, and my final Sunday would be in two weeks. Somewhat in shock, I began to question him.

"Were all the resignations accepted?" I asked.

"No," he responded.

"Was this for moral, disciplinary, or performance reasons?"

"No, Doug."

"Then why?"

"The board and I feel that it serves two purposes," he said. "To give you and Evon time together, and to help ease the pressure on the board to find a pastor for the church, rather than an administrator for the present staff."

"But the other staff—the children's pastor, book-keeper, receptionist—have been retained?"

"Yes."

The next Sunday morning, the pastor announced that all resignations had been declined except mine. He stated that "many would be confused or hurt by this, but that sometimes 'ignorance is bliss.'" I still don't know what he meant by that. I do know that his decision confused us and the church, and the church split after we left.

The church provided a conditional six-month severance pay. We were expected to move to another city in search of a position like most released ministers, but we could not move without losing the medical and social service connections we had established the previous two years.

Two weeks later, I had packed my office—my career—into a dozen boxes. The lives I had worked so hard to mold into Christlikeness were removed from my touch. We were asked not to attend the church. Though some fought for us, their entreaties were ignored. After all the good-byes were said and the tears had been shed, we went to our home and sat on the couch. Alone. Again.

Two months later, Ashli was rushed to ICU and, within days, she died. It would have been natural to call the church and have them gather and pray, but we couldn't call people who did not want us. There were many dear friends who kept in contact, and we did experience Christlike compassion from them as we endured the pain of our daughter's death. Yet our rejection felt like a loss of oxygen. With the exception of those close friends who stood beside us, we had no church to lean on. We sorely needed the comfort of a church family's prayers. We needed to know that in our despair, other folks were faithfully bringing our names before the Father. In short, we needed tremendous support that our few friends couldn't provide alone.

After Ashli died, we decided to have her funeral at a church where a close friend of mine was youth pastor. Calls began coming from the church where I had been let go. They wanted Ashli's funeral to be held there—the church that had ostracized my wife and daughter. The church that had asked us to leave. I couldn't do it. They were angry and hurt that, as they put it, we "would not let them share with us in our pain." I was livid! They had *caused* much of our pain. They had officially ostracized us from our place of worship. They had removed our only source of income and insurance without any clear reason. And now they were angry at us for following their lead and withdrawing into our lonely family unit. Slowly and steadily, resentment and bitterness began to build in my heart toward this church and its leadership.

A War Within

My greatest battles have always been deep within my own heart. I knew that Satan desired for me to suffer spiritually, that these feelings were a method of attack. I also knew that he would do everything in his power to nurture this rising bitterness. But during moments of reflection, I continued to justify my position. *I don't deserve this!* I consoled myself. *They are wrong. They call themselves Christians? Is this what Christ would have done?*

I freely dispensed sentence upon my former colleagues and friends. Evon became a willing participant in these discussions, adding her own bit of venomous reproof. We began to speak sarcastically about the church and the "right foot of fellowship" we had received. We truly became bitter.

Rebuilding Tool

Be careful about what seeds you allow to take root in your heart. They determine the kind of garden you'll get.

Bitterness, I was to learn, is a cancer of the human spirit. With little effort, it seems to spread until it engulfs every area of our lives. Its roots lie deep in selfishness and resentment. It breeds hatred and violence. It is contradictory to everything that God is. But it is also the easy way out when you've been hurt.

Compounding my bitterness at the church was a new hatred—this time for the people I held responsible for my wife and daughter's disease: homosexuals. We learned that a male homosexual's infected blood donation had contaminated my wife. Along with the people who rejected us because of our condition, I hated the people who had promoted its spread.

The People We Love to Hate

A couple of weeks after informing our church of our HIV-positive status, a young man who worked with the youth and children of our church came trembling toward me after an evening service. He was handsome and muscular, usually happy and enthused. But on this evening, his face was stained with tears, and his eyes were puffy and red.

"Can I speak to you, Pastor Doug?" he asked.

"Sure," I said. He motioned for the senior pastor to come join us. We all sat down on the edge of the preaching platform. My friend struggled to compose himself. After a long period of crying, he was finally able to speak.

"Pastor has known for some time that I was involved in homosexuality over a year ago," he said. "I'm not now, but . . ." He began to cry again. My mind raced. I knew what he would say next. "I got tested last week and I . . . just found out that I'm . . . HIV positive!" With this he collapsed in grief.

As I sat there beside him, I knew it would be natural and appropriate for me, his youth pastor, to embrace him and encourage him after this emotionally painful confession. It is what any real Christian would do.

But my mind was torn. As I saw it, homosexuality was the lifestyle that so rapidly spread this foul disease. Had homosexuals not been a factor, this virus most likely would have been contained in its origin, I thought. Instead, their promiscuity had caused a rampage of disease that finally affected two incredibly innocent people: my wife and my daughter.

Because of homosexuals, every time Evon and I became intimate, our spontaneity was crushed and precautions were taken. Because of a homosexual who had given infectious blood, every time we talked of the future our conversation froze. Bitterness and hatred had grown in my heart for homosexuals, who carelessly transmitted this virus to my wife, so that every time she caught a cold, I panicked. I found it easy and justifiable to hate homosexuals and pronounce judgment and a raging hell on them.

But here sat my friend, whom I had loved and worked with for a year. My friend. A homosexual. How could I hate someone I loved?

God was about to pull a switch on me. It started with the challenge my friend offered. I took the bait. I told him, "I love you, and I will be here for you." We embraced.

Rebuilding Tool

The first step away from bitterness seems small but matters most. Take it.

The Turning of the Tide

God wasn't finished. Word of Evon and Ashli's battle with AIDS had become widespread throughout Denver largely due to an article in the *Denver Post*. My wife's best friend, Evelyn, however, worked at a hair salon where several of the hairstylists were gay. They heard of our situation through Evelyn and, since we were patrons of that establishment, embraced us with compassion and acceptance. We were initially hesitant to accept their sympathy, but our hatred began to dissolve as we realized many of them battled the same issues we had: rejection from church, imminent death, grief, and society's ignorance about HIV and AIDS.

Within months after we had left the church and my daughter had died, these homosexual hairstylists approached me about a fund-raiser. They wanted to develop Colorado's first pediatric AIDS foundation. They were working with Denver Children's Hospital and had networked with the hospital's pediatric AIDS group. They asked if they could do some fund-raisers in memory of my daughter. I could tell their empathy was heartfelt, their concern genuine. We consented. And a small, better seed was planted in my heart.

The Ashli Herman Fund existed for years. Networking with other organizations, the men and women behind it have raised tens of thousands of dollars for children with HIV. How could I respond with hate in the face of so much love? These people had "ministered" in the truest sense to my family and to many others. My perspective began to change.

As for my church friend, he was mostly able to maintain his secret. He learned from our experience. For more than a year, he continued to teach Sunday school to the children of our church. He easily strolled into the kitchen my wife was no longer allowed to enter. He saw the compassion from those few who walked with us. He also saw the fear and ignorance that gave birth to rejection and hurt. As a result, he kept mum.

A year after Evon's death, I heard that my friend was hospitalized. I traveled to the Denver hospital to visit him. There lay my friend, frail and weak, breathing with assistance from respiratory devices. His parents had just left, so he was alone. I knew I would never see him again this side of heaven. We talked briefly. I held his hand. I told him how much he meant to our family. Before I left his room, I leaned down and kissed him on the forehead. He died two days later.

When you have looked into the eyes of those you love, knowing that they will soon lie lifeless in a satin-lined casket, you find yourself in a state of possession. By that I mean your desire to be in control and remove the sickness is immense. All that pours out of you is rich compassion. You love with such intensity that your heart feels it may burst. You hold dear the time you have, not wanting to let go. You possess the moment. You want to possess your loved one.

With so great a love in my heart, I found myself tiring from the battle of right and wrong. I didn't want to be bitter any longer. I wanted to love my friends and family. I really wanted to love the church. To do this, I had to release the issues of right and wrong to God and trust his wisdom and justice. I had to value the life that we all share and force myself to keep love in the forefront of all I did.

I overcame my bitterness by choosing to love and not resent first my church friend, then the homosexuals who comforted and supported us, then the church that had abandoned us. The key, I found, was releasing the right I thought I had to harbor judgment and bitterness toward people. I admit that occasionally feelings of resentment arise or I catch myself in a sarcastic dig at the church. But I strive to keep my heart pure and free from the root of bitterness, which destroys our love from within.

We all long to love without hesitation. If you have been through any type of faithquake, you understand how bitterness challenges your every relationship, how your past wounds haunt you. You know the surge of dark inner feelings when you see certain faces at church. Living without bitterness frees our hearts from those heavy chains. A pure heart lets us laugh again, love again. It lets us *live* again.

You may have been there too. It's time to let the pain of the past go and get on with your life. Bitterness and resentment destroy only you, no one else. This is not a simple challenge, but you can do it. First, understand that you exist to glorify God. You are alive because God willed it, and he has a purpose for you. You do not exist to fulfill any agenda of your own.

Second, you must allow yourself to be broken by the Spirit of God. This is where you sacrificially lift your pride to him. As he breaks your heart and you become pliable before him, you release any desire toward vengeance. You must resign your right to these things— they are no longer yours. Any feeling other than compassion for others and submission to God must be sacrificed as well. It is this emptying of yourself that is vital. Christ set the example (Phil. 2:5–11).

Finally, you must live in the constant awareness that this bitterness can and may arise again and again in your heart. Your self-discipline to offer these feelings to God is crucial. It is so easy to choose to walk down the bitter road. But nip it in the bud. Remember, you are his. You can overcome your resentment. Your heart deserves to be better, not bitter.

13

The Final Challenge: Forgiveness

For if you forgive men when they sin against you, your
heavenly Father will also forgive you.

Matthew 6:14

It was a hot Sunday evening in Texas. The humidity pen-
etrated the air-conditioning of the large church building, and several hundred people sat in sticky silence.
Not a sound was made as I presented the truth of God's
Word to them. I passionately expounded on the revolu-
tionary claims of the Bible to change people from the
inside out, replace despair with hope, and restore relationships, starting today.

Then came time for the congregation's response. I
prayed, then offered them the opportunity to come forward and pray together.

No one moved.

My heart churned with ache as I looked at the parish-
ioners shuffling in their seats. I didn't want to keep them
longer than necessary, but I sensed some deep pain

embedded within this congregation. I challenged them again to respond in honesty and love for one another. Still no one moved.

Many preachers tally the success of their preaching on the number of responses at the altar following the sermon. I learned long ago, however, that through simple manipulation and emotional appeal, I could pack the altars. This wasn't success at anything but crowd control. I'd decided early in my ministry to work for genuine response, whether it came in few or no faces at the front. I wasn't looking for a crowd to make me feel good. I did sense real suffering within the members of this church, and I couldn't drop my challenge to them until they moved toward healing.

I made one final plea from the pulpit. "Some people have said to me, 'God can minister to me right where I'm sitting. I don't need to come forward.' Wrong! Of course he can, but he won't. The reason you are not coming forward is because of pride. He can't bless that attitude. Who cares what others think of you? This is between you and God, not you and them. And it doesn't matter to me either. I don't get brownie points for this. I don't make a commission off your response. I don't even get a rush. If you want to walk out that door in ten minutes, you can. And you can face the fear and pain and hurt alone again. But I promise you, you won't make it. It will still haunt you.

"I'm going to wait a few more minutes. I want you to be honest. If you need what I have talked about today, come."

After waiting a few minutes, a few couples got up together and moved toward the area in front of the pulpit. They knelt and began to weep. Soon others began to move forward as well. A swell of people made their way toward the front. All of them were breaking in sorrow. In my heart of hearts, I felt God speak to me. "They are dealing with bitterness and unforgiveness," he said.

I spoke gently to the folks at the front. "Sometimes it's hard to forgive someone when he or she has hurt you deeply. It wasn't your fault. But it wasn't Jesus' fault either, and he forgave. I challenge you with my heart: Will you forgive and let God complete the healing in your soul tonight?"

In the moments following that announcement, others bowed their heads and wept in the pews where they sat. Still others came forward toward the already-full altar area. It was an evening of release and healing. They were beginning to forgive and love again.

Following the service, the youth pastor took me aside and thanked me for my ministry. "What you may not have known, Doug, is that our pastor was caught having an affair with a woman in the church recently. The people here have been deeply hurt and can't seem to forgive him, his family, or each other. No one trusts anybody. This is a real milestone for our church."

I hadn't known. I pray for that pastor and the church that was devastated by his failure. It is hard to forgive someone quickly when you have put your deepest trust in him. Of course man is destined to fail. It is in our carnal nature. Forgiveness is not. That is why it takes such enormous determination to accomplish it in our lives. Furthermore, it's one thing to forgive nonbelievers who hurt us— we don't hold them to the same standards as we do Christians. It's quite another challenge to forgive our family in Christ, because we know they should know better.

It Starts at Home

Two weeks lumbered by after Ashli's death. Bereaved of both daughter and job, Evon and I contemplated through our pain beginning a new ministry of some type. Since my vow to Ashli and our experience with our church, I knew I wanted to educate churches about AIDS and show them how it's possible to respond in compassion. While praying about this decision, I sensed the Holy Spirit speak loudly to my heart. "I will bless you in this ministry, Doug," he seemed to say. "But you first have to forgive the pastors and the church that hurt you."

"No!" I cried. "How could I forgive them? They took away my ministry. They took away my wife's dearest friends and our only sense of support in this city. They rejected us!"

I wrestled with God over this issue for six weeks. During this time of turmoil, all I could hear the Spirit of God saying to me was, "I will bless you if you forgive them."

"No way," I would respond firmly.

You may wonder how I could refuse to forgive after working through my bitterness. To me, they were two different things, although closely tied together. Replacing bitterness with kindness was one thing; I could stop saying nasty things and be friendly toward my former enemies. But forgiving required a further step—that I forget what they had done to me. It also required me to release them from any liability for our pain. That seemed out of the question.

However, God does not easily tire. I did. During the sixth week, I responded to the Lord in brokenness. "Why?" I asked him weakly. "We didn't do anything wrong. Why should we forgive them?"

"I didn't do anything wrong, either," Jesus whispered. "But I forgave. Now, will you be obedient and forgive them, or not?" I was truly broken. This would be the hardest spiritual task that I would ever experience.

My face hot with tears, I knew again I had to follow in his steps. I sat behind my computer and typed out a letter of reconciliation to all the board members and pastors. "If I have personally hurt you, forgive me. . . . I love you. If you desire to respond, that is fine but not necessary. I'll accept your silence as affirmation to our reconciled relationship."

After dropping those nine letters in the post office slot, I sensed a great release. It wasn't just a good feeling but more the dropping of a burden. Everything looked brighter, within and without. It was as if the clouds moved back to reveal a bluer sky.

People have asked me many times about the situation that occurred with that church in Denver. Most people want to know how I could forgive them after they rejected us at such a crucial time of crisis in our lives.

Rebuilding Tool

Like any other new habit, forgiveness takes practice. You only get better the more you work at it.

I don't have a comprehensive answer for that. In one sense, I didn't feel I had a choice. Jesus forgave those who hurt him while he hung in innocence on the cross. And although I am not Christ, I have chosen to follow his example. For me, forgiveness was an issue of obedience. That's the cerebral aspect.

Emotionally, though, I continually wrestle with feelings that arise from that hurt. When these feelings arise, I must practice forgiveness again and again. It is not just letting go of the things they did to us, it is releasing them from the guilt and condemnation I feel they deserve. This is not easy. I have not yet conquered it. But I know it is what I must do.

There's Always One More

I'm convinced I'll never be through learning about forgiveness. Some months later, after Evon's death, I got yet another lesson. I was a thirty-year-old widower with a six-year-old son. Graciously, the Lord fulfilled my desire to speak out against AIDS and its destruction. I began to travel across the nation speaking to churches, high schools, conventions, even making an occasional television or radio appearance.

With my son on the front row at the meetings, I shared our tragedy and pain. I spoke of our battles and my faithfulness to Evon until her final breath. At churches my tears flowed freely as I challenged congregations to love deeply and cherish the life and families they have. I challenged people toward integrity and strength with compassion. These moments created great response following the services.

The ones who exhibited the biggest public response were women. They were not afraid to speak of the questions and pain they too had felt. I soon learned they were also attracted to a man who seemed faithful, strong, and compassionate. And I was single. Many single women came and thanked me for my testimony. One even gave me her phone number after a service and said, "If there is anything you need this weekend, *anything* at all, just call." I quickly realized I could put myself into a dangerous position if I was not careful. I had no idea this faithquake survivor would prove such a magnet for female attention.

Flattered but frightened, I had to admit my loneliness since Evon's death. While I did not want to commit a moral failure, I was torn. Months began to fly by, and I felt my aloneness more and more keenly. Eventually at every venue I spoke in, I found myself looking for the next Mrs. Doug Herman. It almost became habitual. I was hunting for a wife. Not because I truly loved the women I met, but because I was lonely.

Various dating relationships followed. Most of them were very awkward and strained. It was strange enough to be thirty and have to learn to date all over again. But add to that the fact that I travel and speak full time about my late wife and that puts a lot of pressure on a relationship. And, of course, I could never tell the women I dated that I was simply looking for a wife. Whether I loved them or not wasn't the issue then. In fact the women themselves weren't the issue then. I had a position that needed to be filled, and I was trying to fill it.

Needless to say, I hurt many people as well as myself. I allowed my focus to stray from what was truly important to what I wanted. It wasn't a need. I needed to grieve. I wanted a wife. I used dating relationships to escape my grief over Evon, to hide from my pain and loneliness.

A year after Evon had died, I dated several wonderful women. None of the relationships were fulfilling. In fact I was deeply confused. I knew the problem wasn't the women—they were first-class. The problem was that I didn't care about them for who they were, but rather for what I needed, which was companionship, not love. I finally grabbed my Rolodex and found the name of a friend who was a family and marriage therapist. I went to see Larry immediately.

What did he recommend? You guessed it. More forgiveness. This time, though, it was for me. I failed myself. I hadn't given myself enough time to recover from my faithquake to pursue a new family. Now I had to forgive myself.

Larry told me to write a letter describing my feelings of hurt and anger. He also asked me to write a letter of forgiveness to myself. In a powerful counseling session, he placed an empty chair in the room and turned his back to me. He told me to envision myself in the chair and read the letter out loud.

I stumbled. I began to see myself sitting there—smug, slightly arrogant, confident, but damaged. I unloaded my hurt and all the disappointment I felt toward myself. A stream of tears trickled over my chin as I began to tell myself that in spite of all the hurt I had caused, it was okay. "I forgive you, Doug," I said. "I forgive you for your selfishness and I forgive you for your sin." I began to release myself from all the guilt that I had shackled over my heart and soul.

Whether it was the therapeutic cry or the act of forgiveness, I don't know. But I did feel lighter and fresh. I drove home in silence. Going into my bedroom, I looked into the mirror. I smiled. I actually liked the person I saw there.

You may think this is a bit strange. That's okay. All I can say is, it worked. The process of forgiving yourself is not unlike loving yourself. It was Christ who said, "Love your neighbor as yourself." I had offered forgiveness to my neighbors, and now I had to offer it to myself. The result was relief and joy.

> **Give yourself the gift of forgiveness. It's the only way to rebuild without baggage.**
>
> **Rebuilding Tool**

This is an incredibly important tool for rebuilding after faithquake. The acts of forgiving others and yourself are immensely liberating, allowing you to move on emotionally without hindrance. I have met so many who desperately need to forgive themselves for the failures they have allowed in their lives. They made bad choices and they know it. But now it is time to go on. Unless they forgive and release themselves from the condemnation that enslaves them, they will be bound to the failures and disappointments that haunt them.

Yes, it may sound strange. But it is real—powerful. Chances are that if you are scoffing at this concept, you need it the most.

Not Quite Finished

"Doug, you need to forgive God."

"Impossible," I said. "God cannot sin. Therefore, he does not require forgiveness. It's a theological impossibility to forgive God."

My counselor was unshaken by my statement. "Do you *feel* like God hurt you? Regardless of who was at fault, if there was fault, did you experience hurt from God?"

"Yes. Hurt and disappointment."

"Then it may be a theological impossibility, but it is emotionally imperative that you deal with the hurt you feel came from God. For your emotional well-being, you need to forgive and release God from the hurt and disappointment he caused you."

Larry was right. Regardless of our theological training, we are human beings complete with emotional sensors that record pain, no matter its source. I felt that God had let me down. He could have intervened. He could have healed. He could have, but he didn't. That hurt. And deep inside, I held him responsible.

How do you forgive God? The same way you forgive anyone else. It requires sincerity and compassion. It requires the combination of forgiveness and the complete release from his responsibility that caused the hurt.

"Dear Lord," I stuttered. "You could have done something. You let my daughter die and you let Evon die. I know you love them, but . . . that hurt, God! You hurt me and you hurt my son.

"But I want you to know that I love you and I forgive you. I release you from the pain I felt you caused me. I forgive you." As tears trickled down my cheeks, I thanked him for being my God.

Telling God that I forgave him was again very powerful for me. It brought me closer to him as I removed the walls of tense judgment that I had built. Our love became more tangible and dynamic. I quickly learned that without forgiveness, you can't rebuild.

14

A New Foundation

To make an end is to make a beginning. The end is where we start from.

T. S. Eliot

As your faithquake has ended and you have begun to rebuild, do you realize where you're standing? Do you know that you are on the threshold of a brand-new life? Perhaps you really wish you had the old one back. Maybe the idea of fresh adventure not only fails to excite you—it exhausts you. That's okay. It's natural to feel like staying somewhere between "a time to mourn and a time to dance" (Eccles. 3:4). But I suspect you will feel the stirring soon to move on, to find the new life that awaits you.

As I responded to that stirring and dealt with issues of anger and bitterness, the call to growth, and the miracle of humor, I developed some principles. These principles helped me rebuild on a firm foundation. If I am ever shaken by a faithquake again, I know I will remain grounded because of them.

Principles for Rebuilding

1. Whatever is still standing is worth keeping.

Old western movies are wonderfully entertaining if you don't mind seeing the same plot over and over again: bad guy oppresses the innocent; good guy comes to the innocent's defense; bad guy and good guy struggle; and when the smoke clears, good guy stands triumphant—the innocent redeemed. In a sense, that is what happens to us in faithquakes. Something awful and inexplicable happens (bad guy) to us (the innocent); our faith (good guy) comes to help us; the bad guy tries to overwhelm the good guy; the smoke clears, and if we've worked hard and clung to our Savior, a few things remain. We peer through the smoke to see what's left.

After my faithquake, I found mostly rubble. Thankfully, I still had my relationship with God, but lots of inconsequentials had collapsed. What I lost along the way were certain denominational dogmas that had little to do with the certainties of Christ as Savior and Lord, friendships whose mettle couldn't withstand the fire of our adversity, some idealized notions of "prosperity now and always for the believer," my income, and my status. I also lost the arrogant refusal to forgive, the sting of bitterness, and the consuming power of anger. What remained: My certainty that God was who he said he was—loving and strong (Ps. 62:11–12); the love of my son, Josh, and my family; and a little bit of hope that we could do more than survive.

Starting again meant I had to clear the rubble from my foundation. I had to sweep away anything that would hinder my movement forward, even those things I kept "for sentimental reasons." I'm not speaking here of mementos, of keepsakes. I'm speaking of old dreams that my faithquake dashed. The rubble of our lives is not necessarily a keepsake. Those things in our lives that have crumbled we must either restore or remove. Those things that lasted through the shaking we must cling to.

2. Love your memories, but let them remain just that.

You may feel the temptation I felt after Evon's death, to fill your life with memories of life b.f.—Before Faithquake. You may love those experiences so much that you let them halt your future. But they're ultimately unsatisfying because they're intangibles. Nothing can bring back what is lost. Even if you could restore your circumstances, things still wouldn't be the same. Why? Because you are different. A faithquake changes a person—hopefully for the better.

Rebuilding Tool

Use the "shovel of hope" to clear away the rubble of your faithquake.

Make sure the foundation you're building upon isn't cluttered with fond illusions or empty hopes. Please hear me when I say you can't build anything solid on anything less than Jesus Christ himself. You can't build on Jesus *and* cherished dreams you had with someone who is gone. You can't build on Jesus *and* the sometimes unrealistic visions of regaining all you lost. You have to build on Jesus. He stands faithful. He stands true. And he stands alone.

3. Construction starts with a single step and is finished after many steps.

I have a confession to make: I used to dislike the Twenty-third Psalm. Maybe it was because I usually heard it read at funerals and I associated it with death. Recently it has served to challenge me, to give me a new perspective on life and grief. And it has taught me patience while recovering from faithquake.

> Examine your foundation with the "level of truth." Don't build on anything that isn't Jesus Christ.

Rebuilding Tool

Look at that psalm with me for a moment.

The Lord is my shepherd, I shall not be in want.
    He makes me lie down in green pastures,
he leads me beside quiet waters,
    he restores my soul.
He guides me in paths of righteousness
    for his name's sake.
Even though I walk
    through the valley of the shadow of death,
I will fear no evil,
    for you are with me;
your rod and your staff,
    they comfort me.

You prepare a table before me
    in the presence of my enemies.
You anoint my head with oil;
    my cup overflows.
Surely goodness and love will follow me
    all the days of my life,
and I will dwell in the house of the Lord
    forever.

Notice the several locations listed here. We find a meadow and valley with a path running through them, a table, and ultimately the house of the Lord. In the meadow, we find the life of luxury and freedom. Nurture and growth are evident here. But as we follow the path of righteousness, we often find ourselves in the valley of the shadow. We may walk this path through our own struggles or we may walk it with those caught in their own challenges. It is here that we experience faithquake. In this valley, mountains loom before us and winds of change nearly sweep us off our feet. Unlike the broad paths in the meadow, the path in the valley is narrow and filled with obstacles. Sounds of predators send fear into our hearts, and the shadows cause our pulse to quicken. Yet Christ assures us that we are not alone. His rod and staff comfort us.

Near the end of this valley is a banquet table set before our enemies. These are our mortal enemies: death, hell, and the grave. They taunt us arrogantly beside their king, Satan. This table is where we say good-bye to loved ones and allow Christ to comfort us in our loss. He anoints our heads with oil and our cups overflow with perfect peace and blessing as God's children. We are given the power to survive. Beyond this table is the house of the Lord, which we can only glimpse for now, and where we will dwell for all eternity.

I personally escorted my daughter to this table and handed her to our God to take to his eternal home. Eight months later, I held the hand of my wife as we traveled the valley again. I watched as Christ ushered her into his kingdom. Eight months after that, my family traversed the valley yet another time, delivering my brother to that table of peace and his home of promise.

When our loved ones leave us, we must turn and walk back down the valley to the meadow of normal life. We want to remain at the table, but our loved ones are no longer there. We also want to be transported instantly back to the meadow, but this is a process that we must walk patiently. It is the process of grief.

Following your faithquake, you may be grieving the loss of a loved one. It doesn't have to be due to death. Loss can come in many forms. And it doesn't have to be the loss of a person. Financial collapse, rebellion from within your family, rejection from an institution—these can all be vehicles of faithquake. Regardless of what kind of shaking you endured, the fact is, *you endured*. You now have to rebuild your life. And in this rebuilding, you must walk back down the winding path in the valley of the shadow. Memories of the tragedy will flash in your mind as you hear a song, see a restaurant once frequented, or turn to a voice calling your name. This path back to the meadow of peace is longer than anyone desires. But it is the right length and it is necessary.

I vividly remember telling my friends, "I just want to be normal again." What I wanted was to romp and play in the meadows. I wanted out of the valley. I wanted my new life and I wanted it *now*. But it doesn't happen that way.

As both therapy and hobby, I decided to finish two of the four levels of our home. I learned that construction is a process. It must be accomplished one step at a time. I couldn't frame the walls and carpet the floor in the same day. One board at a time, one nail at a time, the walls would take shape. I finished the rooms over ten months.

One ideal at a time, one truth at a time, I have rebuilt my life. I believe many of the same things I did prior to my faithquake, but this time they are anchored to the foundation, not each other. (In other words, I don't maintain beliefs because my denomination demands it, but because I have tested them and found them true.) I have learned to be patient with the painful and frustrating grief process. I have examined the foundation of my faith and have established my life upon the unshakable truth of Jesus Christ.

4. No matter how much you restore, life will never be exactly the same.

When I was a youth pastor years ago, a high school student brought me a gift of a poster one afternoon. The poster reminds us that God is named "I Am." It encourages us not to fret over the past and our failures or live in fear of an uncertain future, but instead learn to touch the God of now.

This poster challenged me for years. We can all fill a page with regrets of our past. Certainly every human has fears of the future. But to learn the powerful truth of the ever-present Jesus Christ is to live in the moment at hand. "Carpe diem!" is the expression we must embrace as a life theme.

Rebuilding Tool

Anchor the structure of your new life to the one unshakable foundation, one board at a time.

Having lost half my family in eight months, I had reason to regret and fear. Yet for some reason—the prayers of hundreds cannot be discounted—I found myself pushing forward into a new life with my young son. I refused to be trapped in the pain and regrets of my faithquake. We began decorating our lives with wonderful new relationships and activities. Joshua and I traveled all over this nation together experiencing a new life. We chose together whom I would date when that time was appropriate. And he gave me the "thumbs up" when I asked what he thought of my marrying Stephanie.

Today, my wife, Stephanie, and my new little girl, Bri, are the sparkle of our household. Joshua and I have endured the extremes of great pain and now bask in the extremes of blessing. I discovered no formula, just the truth conveyed by the poster: God is here in the present. My new life must be established *here*.

When you face the opportunity to rebuild your life, do so with passion and vision. Adorn your life with new relationships and punctuate your heartbeat with creative new activities. This wonderful world God has given us awaits your involvement. Dear friend, lift up your chin and go forward.

> **Rebuilding Tool**
>
> Don't sit in barren rooms of fear and regret. Furnish your life with new relationships and activities.

A Last Word

It would be easy to focus your entire life on the crisis you just survived. We all know people who seem to live in the moment of their catastrophe. But our faithquakes cannot be the focus of our lives and futures. There comes a time to go on.

God is not through with us yet! We are breathing for a reason. Let the faithquake experience be only a memory filled with emotions and wisdom gleaned for others.

Remember where we started? "To this you were called, because Christ suffered for you, leaving you an example, that you should follow in his steps" (1 Peter 2:21). You have followed in his steps of suffering—now you can follow in his steps to resurrection. Rebuild on him.

Notes

Chapter 3: *The Calling*

1. Philip Yancey, *Disappointment with God: 3 Questions No One Asks Aloud* (Grand Rapids: Zondervan, 1988), 186.

Chapter 7: *Stand Firm*

1. Dr. Paul Brand and Philip Yancey, *In His Image* (Grand Rapids: Zondervan, 1984), 94–95.
2. Ibid., 95.

Chapter 9: *When Everything You Believe Is Shaken*

1. W. C. Martin and Daniel B. Towner, "My Anchor Holds," *Hymns of Glorious Praise* (Springfield, Mo.: Gospel Publishing House, 1969), 297.

Doug Herman is an international speaker and author who has spent over twenty years in youth and family work. Forums in which he has displayed his speaking ability include school systems, businesses, parent and family conferences, fund-raising banquets, and religious organizations and events.

Currently, Doug speaks to over 250,000 teens and adults yearly about character development, sexual abstinence, and spiritual passion. He is the founder of Integrated Community Events, Inc., a nonprofit organization linking community networks for strategic efforts. The Pure Revolution Project is one of those efforts created by Doug to bring the message of sexual postponement until marriage to students, families, and communities.

Doug has been a youth pastor at small country churches as well as one of the nation's largest multicultural churches. His experience as a high school coach and substitute teacher has aided his effectiveness in the high school assembly programs he conducts nationally every year. Doug has been seen and heard on over one hundred various national radio and television programs and has published articles in *Leadership Journal, Youthworker, Living with Teenagers,* and *ParentLife.*

Doug's new radio program, *Pure Revolution,* debuted in June 2002 on 313 stations. To learn more, visit Doug's web site: www.purerevolution.com.

ALSO BY
DOUG HERMAN

WHAT GOOD
IS GOD?

Finding Faith and Hope
in Troubled Times

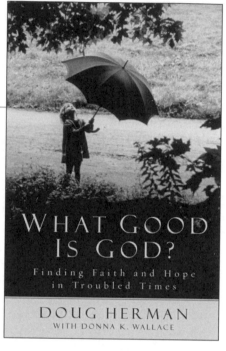

**Have you ever wondered
if God is good?**

One minute you're strolling
peacefully down life's path,
and the next minute—you're
hit suddenly by an illness,
a broken relationship, an
unexpected tragedy, or an
emotional upheaval. In those
times, we're often barraged
with doubts about God: If
you're good, why do I hurt so
much? If you're there, why are
you silent? If you love me, why don't you help me? What good are you?

After author Doug Herman buried his wife, baby daughter, and brother
all within a few short months, he pounded heaven with those very questions. The answers—both life empowering and bubbling with hope—
are found in *What Good Is God?*

Touching on Doug's experiences as well as a wealth of biblical and
contemporary stories, this engaging book powerfully testifies that God
can see you through your deepest pain. Each page asserts the truth:
Even in life's hardest storms, God is good.

Whether for yourself or a hurting friend, *What Good Is God?* offers sol-
ace during hard times and a message of hope, comfort, and truth for all
travelers who find their path dipping into the valley of shadows.